CBSE Term II
2022

Business Studies

Class XI

CBSE Term II 2022

Business Studies

Class XI

- Complete Theory Covering NCERT
- Case Based Questions
- Short/Long Answer Type Questions
- 3 Practice Papers with Explanations

Author
Aman Sharma

arihant

ARIHANT PRAKASHAN (School Division Series)

ARIHANT PRAKASHAN (School Division Series)

© **Publisher**

No part of this publication may be re-produced, stored in a retrieval system or by any means, electronic, mechanical, photocopying, recording, scanning, web or otherwise without the written permission of the publisher. Arihant has obtained all the information in this book from the sources believed to be reliable and true. However, Arihant or its editors or authors or illustrators don't take any responsibility for the absolute accuracy of any information published and the damage or loss suffered thereupon.

All disputes subject to Meerut (UP) jurisdiction only.

卐 **Administrative & Production Offices**

Regd. Office
'Ramchhaya' 4577/15, Agarwal Road, Darya Ganj, New Delhi -110002
Tele: 011- 47630600, 43518550

卐 **Head Office**
Kalindi, TP Nagar, Meerut (UP) - 250002, Tel: 0121-7156203, 7156204

卐 **Sales & Support Offices**
Agra, Ahmedabad, Bengaluru, Bareilly, Chennai, Delhi, Guwahati, Hyderabad, Jaipur, Jhansi, Kolkata, Lucknow, Nagpur & Pune.

卐 **ISBN :** 978-93-25796-78-2

PO No : TXT-XX-XXXXXXX-X-XX

Published by Arihant Publications (India) Ltd.

For further information about the books published by Arihant, log on to www.arihantbooks.com or e-mail at info@arihantbooks.com

Follow us on 

Contents

Watch Free Learning Videos

Subscribe **arihant** You Tube Channel

- ☑ Video Solutions of CBSE Sample Papers
- ☑ Chapterwise Important MCQs
- ☑ CBSE Updates

Syllabus

CBSE Term II Class XI

Theory - 40 Marks   **Duration - 2 hrs**

PART B : FINANCE AND TRADE		Periods	Marks
7.	Sources of Business Finance	28	20
8.	Small Business and Entrepreneurship Development	16	
9.	Internal Trade	22	20
10.	International Business	04	
	Total	**70**	**40**
	Project Work (Part - 2)		**10**

PART B **FINANCE AND TRADE**

Unit 7: Sources of Business Finance

Business finance: Concept and Importance	• State the meaning, nature and importance of business finance.
Owners' funds- equity shares, preferences share, retained earnings, Global Depository receipt (GDR), American Depository Receipt (ADR) and International Depository Receipt (IDR) – concept	• Classify the various sources of funds into owners' funds. • State the meaning of owners' funds. • Understand the meaning of Global Depository receipts, American Depository Receipts and International Depository Receipts.
Borrowed funds: debentures and bonds, loan from financial institution and commercial banks, public deposits, trade credit and	• State the meaning of borrowed funds. • Discuss the concept of debentures, bonds, loans from financial institutions and commercial banks, Trade credit • Distinguish between owners' funds and borrowed funds.

Unit 8: Small Business and Entrepreneurship Development

Entrepreneurship Development (ED): Concept and Need. Process of Entrepreneurship Development: Start-up India Scheme, ways to fund startup. Intellectual Property Rights and Entrepreneurship	• Understand the concept and need of Entrepreneurship Development (ED), Intellectual Property Rights • Understand the process of Entrepreneurship Development
Small scale enterprise – Definition	• Understand the definition of small enterprises
Role of small business in India with special reference to rural areas	• Discuss the role of small scale business in India with special reference to rural areas
Government schemes and agencies for small scale industries: National Small Industries Corporation (NSIC) and District Industrial Centre (DIC) with special reference to rural, backward areas	• Appreciate various schemes of NSIC and DIC with special reference to rural, backward area.

Unit 9: Internal Trade

Internal trade - meaning and types of services rendered by a wholesaler and a retailer	• State the meaning and types of internal trade. • Appreciate the services of wholesalers and retailers.
Large scale retailers-Departmental stores, chain stores – concept	• Highlight the distinctive features of departmental stores, chain stores

Unit 10: International Trade

International trade: concept and benefits	• Understand the concept of international trade. • Describe the benefit of international trade to the nation and business firms.

PROJECT WORK IN BUSINESS STUDIES (ONLY ONE PROJECT): GUIDELINES AS GIVEN IN CLASS XII CURRICULUM

CBSE Circular

Acad – 51/2021, 05 July 2021

Exam Scheme Term I & II

केन्द्रीय माध्यमिक शिक्षा बोर्ड
(शिक्षा मंत्रालय, भारत सरकार के अधीन एक स्वायत संगठन)
CENTRAL BOARD OF SECONDARY EDUCATION
(An Autonomous Organisation under the Ministryof Education, Govt. of India)

Special Scheme for 2021-22

A. Academic session to be divided into 2 Terms with approximately 50% syllabus in each term:

The syllabus for the Academic session 2021-22 will be divided into 2 terms by following a systematic approach by looking into the interconnectivity of concepts and topics by the Subject Experts and the Board will conduct examinations at the end of each term on the basis of the bifurcated syllabus. This is done to increase the probability of having a Board conducted classes X and XII examinations at the end of the academic session.

B. The syllabus for the Board examination 2021-22 will be rationalized similar to that of the last academic session to be notified in July 2021. For academic transactions, however, schools will follow the curriculum and syllabus released by the Board vide Circular no. F.1001/CBSE-Acad/Curriculum/2021 dated 31 March 2021. Schools will also use alternative academic calendar and inputs from the NCERT on transacting the curriculum.

C. Efforts will be made to make Internal Assessment/ Practical/ Project work more credible and valid as per the guidelines and Moderation Policy to be announced by the Board to ensure fair distribution of marks.

Details of Curriculum Transaction

- Schools will continue teaching in distance mode till the authorities permit in-person mode of teaching in schools.

- **Classes IX-X: Internal Assessment** (throughout the year-irrespective of Term I and II) would include the *3 periodic tests, student enrichment, portfolio and practical work/ speaking listening activities/ project.*

- **Classes XI-XII: Internal Assessment** (throughout the year-irrespective of Term I and II) would include end of topic or unit tests/ exploratory activities/ practicals/ projects.

- Schools would create a student profile for all assessment undertaken over the year and retain the evidences in digital format.

- CBSE will facilitate schools to upload marks of Internal Assessment on the CBSE IT platform.

- Guidelines for Internal Assessment for all subjects will also be released along with the rationalized term wise divided syllabus for the session 2021-22.The Board would also provide additional resources like sample assessments, question banks, teacher training etc. for more reliable and valid internal assessments.

केन्द्रीय माध्यमिक शिक्षा बोर्ड

(शिक्षा मंत्रालय, भारत सरकार के अधीन एक स्वायत संगठन)

CENTRAL BOARD OF SECONDARY EDUCATION

(An Autonomous Organisation under the Ministryof Education, Govt. of India)

Term I Examinations:

- At the end of the first term, the Board will organize **Term I Examination** in a flexible schedule to be conducted between November-December 2021 with a window period of 4-8 weeks for schools situated in different parts of country and abroad. Dates for conduct of examinations will be notified subsequently.

- The Question Paper will have Multiple Choice Questions (MCQ) including case-based MCQs and MCQs on assertion-reasoning type. Duration of test will be **90 minutes** and it will cover only the rationalized syllabus of **Term I only** (i.e. approx. 50% of the entire syllabus).

- Question Papers will be sent by the CBSE to schools along with marking scheme.

- The exams will be conducted under the supervision of the External Center Superintendents and Observers appointed by CBSE.

- The responses of students will be captured on OMR sheets which, after scanning may be directly uploaded at CBSE portal or alternatively may be evaluated and marks obtained will be uploaded by the school on the very same day. The final direction in this regard will be conveyed to schools by the Examination Unit of the Board.

- Marks of the **Term I** Examination will contribute to the final overall score of students.

Term II Examination/ Year-end Examination:

- At the end of the second term, the Board would organize **Term II or Year-end Examination** based on the rationalized syllabus of Term II only (i.e. approximately 50% of the entire syllabus).

- This examination would be held around **March-April 2022** at the examination centres fixed by the Board.

- The paper will be of **2 hours duration** and have questions of different formats (case-based/ situation based, open ended- short answer/ long answer type).

- In case the situation is not conducive for normal descriptive examination **a 90 minute MCQ based exam** will be conducted at the end of the Term II also.

- Marks of the Term II Examination would contribute to the final overall score.

To cover this situation, we have given both MCQs and Subjective Questions in each Chapter.

केन्द्रीय माध्यमिक शिक्षा बोर्ड
(शिक्षा मंत्रालय, भारत सरकार के अधीन एक स्वायत संगठन)
CENTRAL BOARD OF SECONDARY EDUCATION
(An Autonomous Organisation under the Ministryof Education, Govt. of India)

6. <u>**Assessment / Examination as per different situations**</u>

   A. **In case the situation of the pandemic improves and students are able to come to schools or centres for taking the exams.**

   Board would conduct Term I and Term II examinations at schools/centres and the theory marks will be distributed equally between the two exams.

   B. **In case the situation of the pandemic forces complete closure of schools during November-December 2021, but Term II exams are held at schools or centres.**

   Term I MCQ based examination would be done by students online/offline from home - in this case, the weightage of this exam for the final score would be reduced, and weightage of Term II exams will be increased for declaration of final result.

   C. **In case the situation of the pandemic forces complete closure of schools during March-April 2022, but Term I exams are held at schools or centres.**

   Results would be based on the performance of students on Term I MCQ based examination and internal assessments. The weightage of marks of Term I examination conducted by the Board will be increased to provide year end results of candidates.

   D. **In case the situation of the pandemic forces complete closure of schools and Board conducted Term I and II exams are taken by the candidates from home in the session 2021-22.**

   Results would be computed on the basis of the Internal Assessment/Practical/Project Work and Theory marks of Term-I and II exams taken by the candidate from home in Class X / XII subject to the moderation or other measures to ensure validity and reliability of the assessment.

   In all the above cases, data analysis of marks of students will be undertaken to ensure the integrity of internal assessments and home based exams.

Dr. Joseph Emmanuel
Director (Academics)

PART B

Finance and Trade

CHAPTER 1

Sources of Business Finance

In this Chapter...

- Meaning of Business Finance
- Owner's Funds
- Borrowed Funds

Meaning of Business Finance

The requirement of funds by business to carry out its various activities is called business finance. It is basically concerned with acquisition of funds, use of funds and distribution of profits by a business enterprise.

Nature of Business Finance

- The concept of business finance is very wide and is used in every type of business house.
- It includes all types of funds needed to start, run, expand and diversify the business.
- The primary goal of business finance is to increase the corporate value.

Importance of Business Finance

1. **Necessary to Start Business** Every new venture needs finance to buy plant and machinery, land and building, raw material, etc.
2. **Necessary to Face Economic Cycle** During recession and depression, business needs finance to overcome problems of decreased profitability.
3. **Necessary for Growth** A company needs significant financial investment to acquire new capital, staff or inventory to fuel the growth.
4. **Necessary for the Payments of Debts** Prompt payment of debts can be possible only because of adequate arrangement of finance.
5. **Necessary for Availing the Opportunities** Business can take the advantage of opportunities to earn more, only if it has adequate finance at its disposal.

Financial Needs of Business

The financial needs of the business can be categorised into the following

1. Fixed Capital Requirements

To start a business, fixed assets such as land, plant, machinery, etc are required. The amount which is required to purchase these assets is known as fixed capital requirements of the enterprise. The following points should be remembered regarding fixed capital requirements

- Fixed capital requirements are more for a manufacturing firm as compared to a trading firm.
- Fixed capital requirements are more for a business operating on a large scale.
- Fixed capital requirements should be financed through long-term sources of finance.

2. Working Capital Requirements

A business also needs finance to carry out the various routine activities such as purchase of raw material, payment of electricity bill, rent, etc. The amount required to meet these needs is known as the working capital requirements of the business. The following points should be kept in mind regarding the working capital requirements

- The shorter the operating cycle, the lesser will be the amount of working capital required and vice-versa.
- Working capital requirements are generally met through short-term sources of finance.
- Working capital requirement for a business selling goods on credit or having slow sales turnover is more than otherwise.
- Working capital requirement increases during festive season, expansion of business, shifting to a new location and payments of current debts.

Classification of Sources of Finance

Sources of funds can be classified on the basis of period, ownership and source of generation, as illustrated in the chart below

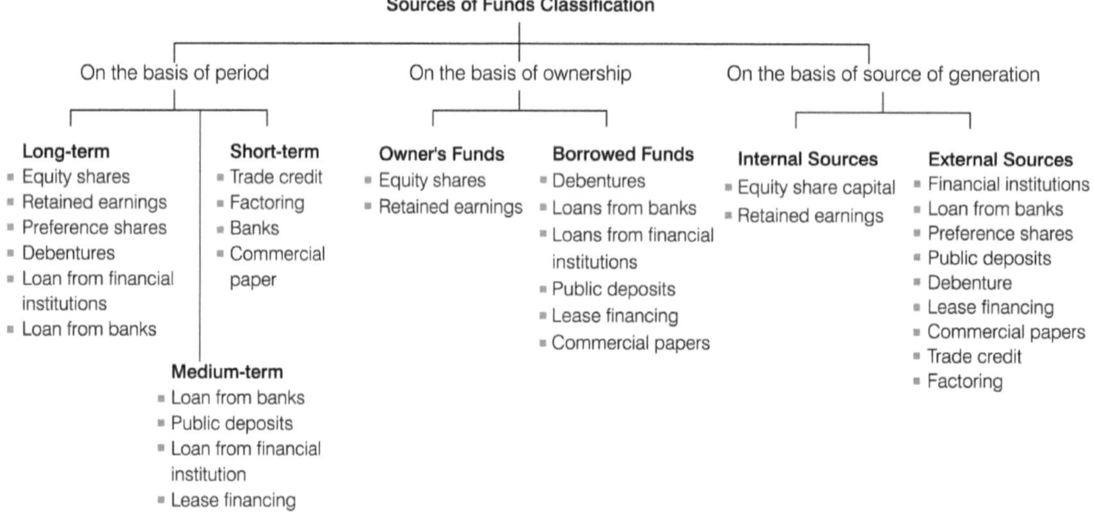

The broad classification of these sources have been discussed ahead.

Classification on the Basis of Period

On this basis of period, sources of funds can be classified as

1. **Long-term Sources** These sources provide finance to business firms for a period exceeding five years.
2. **Medium-term Sources** These sources provide finance to business firms for a period exceeding one year but less than five years.
3. **Short-term Sources** These sources provide finance to business firms for less than one year.

Classification on the Basis of Ownership

On this basis of ownership, sources of funds can be classified as

1. **Owner's Funds** Funds or finance provided by the owners of the business is referred to as owner's funds.
2. **Borrowed Funds** The funds that are raised by way of loans and credit from the public, banks and financial institutions are termed as borrowed funds.

Classification on the Basis of Source of Generation

On the basis of source of generation, sources of funds can be classified as

1. **Internal Sources** These include all those funds which are generated from within a business, such as, from collection of receivables, disposing off surplus inventories and ploughing back of profit. These sources can however, fulfil only limited needs.
2. **External Sources** These include all those funds which are generated from outside a business. These sources carry a cost but large amounts can be raised through these sources.

Owner's Funds

Funds or finance provided by the owners of the business is referred to as owner's funds. Owner's fund include

- Equity Shares
- Preference Shares
- Retained Earnings
- Global Depository Receipt (GDR)/International Depository Receipt (IDR)
- American Depository Receipt (ADR)

Equity Shares

The capital obtained by issue of shares is known as share capital. Equity share capital is a prerequisite to the creation of a company. Equity shareholders do not get a fixed dividend but are paid on the basis of earnings by the company. They are known as the residual owner of the business.

Merits of Equity Shares

- Equity shares are suitable for investors who are willing to assume risk for higher returns.
- There is no burden on the company to pay the dividend.
- Equity capital serves as permanent capital as it is to be repaid only at the time of liquidation of a company.
- Equity capital provides credit worthiness to the company.
- Funds can be raised through equity issue without creating any charge on the assets of the company.

Demerits of Equity Shares

- Equity shares get fluctuating returns.
- The cost of equity shares is generally more as compared to the other sources of funds.
- Issue of additional equity shares dilutes the voting power of existing equity shareholders.
- More formalities and procedural delays are involved while raising funds through issue of equity shares.

Preference Shares

The preference shares give preference shareholders following two rights

- Right to receive a fixed rate of dividend, out of the net profits of the company, before any dividend is declared for equity shareholders.
- Right to receive their capital after the claims of the company's creditors have been settled, at the time of liquidation.

Merits of Preference Shares

- Preference shares provide reasonably steady income in the form of fixed rate of return.
- It does not affect the control of equity shareholders over the management.

- Payment of fixed rate of dividend to preference shares may enable a company to declare higher rates of dividend for the equity shareholders.
- Preference shareholders have a preferential right of repayment over equity shareholders.
- Preference capital does not create any sort of charge against the assets of a company.

Demerits of Preference Shares

- Preference shares are not suitable for those investors who are willing to take risk.
- Preference capital dilutes the claims of equity shareholders over assets of the company.
- The rate of dividend on preference shares is generally higher than the rate of interest on debentures.
- These shares may not be very attractive to the investors as the dividend on these shares is to be paid only when the company earns profit.
- There is no tax saving as dividend paid is not deductible from profits as expense.

Retained Earnings

A portion of the net earnings retained in the business for use in the future is known as retained earnings. This is also referred to as 'ploughing back of profits'.

Merits of Retained Earnings

- Retained earnings is a permanent source of funds.
- It does not involve any explicit cost in the form of interest, dividend or floatation cost.
- There is a greater degree of operational freedom and flexibility.
- It enhances the capacity of the business to absorb unexpected losses.
- It may lead to increase in the market price of the equity shares.

Demerits of Retained Earnings

- Dissatisfaction amongst the shareholders as they would get lower dividends.
- It is an uncertain source of funds as the profits of business are fluctuating.
- The opportunity cost associated with these funds is not recognised by many firms.

Global Depository Receipts (GDRs)/ International Depository Receipts (IDRs)

The local currency shares of a company are delivered to the depository bank. The depository bank issues depository receipts against these shares. Such depository receipts denominated in US dollars are known as Global Depository Receipts (GDR).

GDR is an instrument issued abroad by an Indian company to raise funds in some foreign currency and is listed and traded on a foreign stock exchange.

American Depository Receipts (ADRs)

The depository receipts issued by a company in the USA are known as American Depository Receipts. It is similar to a GDR except that it can be issued only to American citizens and can be listed and traded on a stock exchange of USA.

Borrowed Funds

The funds that are raised from external funds by way of loans and credit from the public, banks and financial institutions are termed as borrowed funds. Borrowed funds include

- Debentures and bonds
- Loan from financial institutions
- Loan from commercial banks
- Public deposits
- Trade credit

Debentures and Bonds

Debenture issued by a company is an acknowledgment that the company has borrowed a certain amount of money, which it promises to repay at a future date. Debenture holders are paid a fixed stated amount of interest at specified intervals say six months or one year.

Bonds are also loan instruments and resemble debentures in all aspects except one i.e., no pre-determined rate of interest is announced at the time of issuing bonds, but a specific rate of interest is announced while issuing debentures.

Merits of Debentures

- It is preferred by investors who want fixed income at lesser risk.
- Debentures are fixed charge funds and do not participate in profits of the company.
- The issue of debentures is suitable in the situation when the sales and earnings are relatively stable.
- Financing through debentures does not dilute control of equity shareholders on management.
- Financing through debentures is less costly as compared to cost of preference or equity capital.

Demerits of Debentures

- As fixed charge instruments, debentures put a permanent burden on the earnings of a company.
- In case of redeemable debentures, the company has to make provisions for repayment on the specified date.
- With the issue of debentures, the capacity of a company to further borrow funds reduces.

Loan from Financial Institutions

The financial institutions established by the central as well as state governments provide both owned capital and loan capital for long and medium term requirements. This source of financing is considered suitable when large funds for longer duration are required for expansion, reorganisation and modernisation of an enterprise.

Merits of Loan from Financial Institutions

- Financial institutions provide long-term finance, which are not provided by commercial banks.
- Many of these institutions provide financial, managerial and technical advice and consultancy to business firms.
- Obtaining loan from financial institutions increase the goodwill of the borrowing company in the capital market.
- It is not a burden on the business as repayment of loan can be made in easy instalments.
- The funds are made available even during periods of depression, when other sources of finance are not available.

Demerits of Loan from Financial Institutions

- Financial institutions follow rigid criteria, many formalities, time and money consuming procedures for grant of loans.
- Certain restrictions such as restriction on dividend payment are imposed by the financial institutions.
- Financial institutions may have their nominees on the board of directors of the borrowing company thereby restricting the powers of the company.

Special Financial Institutions

- Industrial Finance Corporation of India (IFCI)
- State Financial Corporations (SFCs)
- Industrial Credit and Investment Corporation of India (ICICI)
- Industrial Development Bank of India (IDBI)
- State Industrial Development Corporation (SIDCs)
- Unit Trust of India (UTI)
- Industrial Investment Bank of India Ltd. (IIBI)
- Life Insurance Corporation of India (LIC)

Loan from Commercial Banks

Banks extend loans to firms of all sizes and in many ways, like, cash credits, overdrafts, term loans, purchase/discounting of bills and issue of letter of credit. The rate of interest charged by banks depends on various factors such as the characteristics of the firm and the level of interest rates in the economy. Such loans are used for medium to short periods.

Merits of Loan from Commercial Banks

- Banks provide timely assistance to business by providing funds as and when needed by it.
- Secrecy of business can be maintained as the information supplied to the bank by the borrowers is kept confidential.

- Formalities such as issue of prospectus and underwriting are not required for raising loans from a bank.
- Loan from a bank is a flexible source of finance as the loan amount can be increased according to business needs.

Demerits of Loan from Commercial Banks

- Funds are generally available for short periods.
- Banks make detailed investigation of the company's affairs, financial structure etc., and may also ask for security of assets and personal sureties.
- In some cases, difficult terms and conditions are imposed by banks for the grant of loan.

Public Deposits

The deposits that are raised by organisations directly from the public are known as public deposits. Rates of interest offered on public deposits are usually higher than that offered on bank deposits. Public deposits can take care of both medium and short-term financial requirements of a business. The acceptance of public deposits is regulated by the Reserve Bank of India.

Merits of Public Deposits

- The procedure of obtaining deposits is simple.
- Cost of public deposits is generally lower than the cost of borrowings from banks and financial institutions.
- Public deposits do not usually create any charge on the assets of the company.
- The control of the company is not diluted as the depositors do not have voting rights.

Demerits of Public Deposits

- New companies generally find it difficult to raise funds through public deposits.
- It is an unreliable source of finance as the public may not respond when the company needs money.
- Collection of public deposits may prove difficult in case of the size of deposits required is large.

Trade Credit

Trade credit is the credit extended by one trader to another for the purchase of goods and services. Such credit appears in the records of the buyer of goods as 'sundry creditors' or 'accounts payable'. Trade credit is commonly used by business organisations as a source of short-term financing.

Merits of Trade Credit

- Trade credit is a convenient and continuous source of funds.
- Trade credit may be readily available in case the credit worthiness of the customers is known to the seller.
- Trade credit helps to promote the sales of an organisation.
- Trade credit can be availed in situation when any firm wants to increase its existing inventory levels to a higher level.
- It does not create any charge on the assets of the firm while providing funds.

Demerits of Trade Credit

- Availability of easy and flexible trade credit facilities may induce a firm to indulge in overtrading.
- Only limited amount of funds can be generated through trade credit.
- It is generally a costly source of funds.

Difference between Owners' Funds and Borrowed Funds

Basis	Owner's Funds	Borrowed Funds
Meaning	It comprises the funds contributed by the owners and the amount of profit reinvested by them in the business.	It comprises funds taken in the form of loans and advances from other parties.
Nature	It is a permanent source of finance.	It is not a permanent source of finance.
Risk	It is subject to the risks of the business, therefore it is referred to as risk capital.	It is not subject to the risks of the business. Loans are required to be repaid also in case of losses.
Control	The owners of these funds control the affairs of the company.	The owners of these funds have no say in the affairs of the company.
Reward	Owner's funds earn rewards in the form of share in profit, as in the form of dividend.	Borrowed funds earn rewards in the form of interest.
Security	These funds are raised without providing for security of assets.	These funds are raised on security of assets.
Order of Payment	They rank last in the order of payment.	They have priority in the order of payment.
Nature of Obligation	The obligation of payment of return is not fixed.	The obligation of payment of return is fixed.
Rate of Return	The rate of return is not fixed on owner's funds. It fluctuates year after year.	The rate of return on borrowed funds is fixed.

Chapter Practice

Objective Questions

• Multiple Choice Questions

1. Requirement of funds by business to carry out its various activities is known as
(a) business management
(b) business finance
(c) business budgeting
(d) financial management

Ans. (b) A business requires funds for each and every activity from its commencement till it's winding up. This requirement of funds is known as business finance.

2. Primary goal of business finance is to
(a) increase corporate value
(b) increase brand value
(c) reduce debt burden
(d) avail opportunities

Ans. (a) Increase in brand value, reduction of debt burden and availing opportunities are the secondary goals of business finance, while primary goal is to increase corporate value.

3. Fixed capital requirements of a manufacturing concern are
(a) same as that of a trading concern
(b) more than that of a trading concern
(c) less than that of a trading concern
(d) None of the above

Ans. (b) Fixed capital requirements of a manufacturing concern are more since they require more machine and other factory tools as compared to trading concerns.

4. The working capital requirements of a business is high if ......
(a) sales turnover of business is high
(b) it sells goods on credit
(c) it has any expansion plans
(d) All of the above

Ans. (d) All the mentioned options lead to more requirement of working capital majorly in the form of high inventory levels, high outflow of cash and low inflow of cash.

5. Funds needed for the day-to-day operations is called .... capital of the company.
(a) fixed
(b) loan
(c) permanent
(d) working

Ans. (d) working

6. In order to avoid failure in non-payment, fixed capital requirements should be met through which type of source of finance?
(a) Long-term sources
(b) Short-term sources
(c) Medium-term sources
(d) None of the above

Ans. (a) Long-term source of finance gives more opportunity to the borrower to repay the debt thereby helping in avoiding the failure of non-repayment.

7. Mary owns a small farm to grow fruits. She wants to purchase neighbouring land and convert it to farm for increasing the variety of fruits. She wishes to take tractor and some other machine for the same. She will also need money to purchase the land. Which source of finance is required by Mary?
(a) Short-term
(b) Medium-term
(c) Long-term
(d) Both (a) and (b)

Ans. (c) Mary will be able to pay only when her new farm starts giving high quantity of fruits which will require long time, therefore, she requires long-term finance.

8. **Statement I** Medium-term funds remain invested in a business for more than 1 year but less than 5 years.

Statement II Payment of dividend on equity shares is compulsory.

Alternatives
(a) Statement I is correct and statement II is wrong
(b) Statement II is correct and Statement I is wrong
(c) Both the statements are correct
(d) Both the statements are incorrect

Ans. (a) Equity shareholders are the residual owners of the company. So, dividend is only paid when amount is left after making payment to all other liabilities.

9. Directors of X Ltd wants to expand the company, for this they need land, new factory shed and machines.

Being the financial advisor of the company which source from the following you will recommend them?

(a) Debentures
(b) Inter-corporate deposits
(c) Loan from commercial banks
(d) Equity shares

Ans. (d) Acquisition of land and construction of factory shed on it takes time. This means that the factory will not generate any revenues for that time period. Therefore, funds required for the construction of the factory should be arranged from sources which are of long-term and do not require fixed interest payments. Debentures requires fixed interest payment while inter-corporate deposits and loans from commercial banks are short-term in nature. Therefore, equity is the best option among the given options.

10. Equity share capital represents
(a) fixed capital of the company
(b) loan capital of the company
(c) permanent capital of the company
(d) fluctuating capital of the company

Ans. (c) Equity shares are permanent source of capital which are redeemed only at the winding up of the company.

11. **Statement I** Participating preference shares participate in the management of the company.

Statement II The owner funds are a permanent source of finance.

Alternatives

(a) Statement I is correct and statement II is wrong
(b) Statement II is correct and Statement I is wrong
(c) Both the statements are correct
(d) Both the statements are incorrect

Ans. (b) Participating preference shares can participate for additional dividend of the company. They cannot take part in the management of the company.

12. Instead of distributing entire profits to the owners in the form of dividend, some profits are re-invested in business in order to finance the future earnings of the business. This is known as ....

(a) ploughing back   (b) dividend
(c) working capital   (d) dividend stripping

Ans. (a) ploughing back

13. **Statement I** Retained earnings involve any explicit cost in the form of interest, dividend or floatation cost.

Statement II Retained earnings are an uncertain source of fund.

Alternatives

(a) Statement I is correct and statement II is wrong
(b) Statement II is correct and Statement I is wrong
(c) Both the statements are correct
(d) Both the statements are incorrect

Ans. (d) Retained earnings do not involve any explicit cost as it does not involve any form of interest, dividend or floatation cost. As the profits of business are fluctuating, it is an uncertain source of fund.

14. Non-payment of debts on time results in
(a) higher interest costs   (b) loss of goodwill
(c) fines and penalties   (d) All of these

Ans. (d) Non-payment of debts on time results in imposition of fines or penalties by the lender. In normal course of business, money is borrowed at compound interest rates which means interest is charged on interest therefore, if there is any delay in repayment, interest costs would be higher. Extraordinary delay may also result in court cases leading to loss of goodwill.

15. Unsecured debentures are also known as .... debentures.
(a) simple   (b) naked
(c) collateralised   (d) Both (a) and (b)

Ans. (d) Both (a) and (b)

16. The depository receipts issued by the company in the USA are known as ....
(a) GDR   (b) ADR
(c) FDR   (d) Both (b) and (c)

Ans. (b) ADR

17. One of the demerits of loan from financial institutions is that, financial institutions may put ...... in the board of directors of the borrowing company which restricts their power.
(a) independent directors
(b) nominee directors
(c) experts
(d) auditors

Ans. (b) nominee directors

18. Companies generally invites public deposits for a period up to
(a) 5 years   (b) 3 years
(c) 4 years   (d) 10 years

Ans. (b) 3 years

19. **Statement I** In certain situations, collection of public deposits is difficult.

Statement II The dividends to be paid to the preference shareholders are fluctuating.

Alternatives

(a) Statement I is correct and statement II is wrong
(b) Statement II is correct and Statement I is wrong
(c) Both the statements are correct
(d) Both the statements are incorrect

Ans. (a) Collection of public deposits may prove difficult, when the size of deposits required is large. The dividends to be paid to the preference shareholders are fixed.

20. ……is the credit extended by one trader to another for the purchase of goods and services.

   (a) Loan   (b) Trade Credit

   (c) Trade Loan   (d) Both (a) and (b)

Ans. (b) Trade Credit

• Assertion–Reasoning MCQs

Directions (Q. Nos. 1 to 7) *There are two statements marked as Assertion (A) and Reason (R). Read the statements and choose the appropriate option from the options given below*

   (a) Both Assertion (A) and Reason (R) are true and Reason (R) is the correct explanation of Assertion (A)

   (b) Both Assertion (A) and Reason (R) are true, but Reason (R) is not the correct explanation of Assertion (A)

   (c) Assertion (A) is true, but Reason (R) is false

   (d) Assertion (A) is false, but Reason (R) is true

1. **Assertion** (A) The procedure of obtaining funds from commercial banks is complex.

   Reason (R) Banks make detailed investigation of the company's affairs, financial structure, etc. Interest charged by banks depends upon a number of factors, such as nature of advance, period for which the loan is taken, etc.

Ans. (a) Both Assertion (A) and Reason (R) are true and Reason (R) is the correct explanation of Assertion (A).

2. **Assertion** (A) Financing through debentures is less costly.

   Reason (R) Debentures do not carry voting rights. Therefore, financing through debentures does not dilute the control of equity shareholders on management.

Ans. (b) The interest paid on debentures is admissible as an expense according to the provisions of income tax. This helps a company to reduce its tax liability. Therefore, financing through debentures is less costly.

3. **Assertion** (A) Payment of dividend on equity shares is compulsory.

   Reason (R) Voting rights are conferred upon equity shareholders and they participate in the affairs of the business.

Ans. (d) Equity shareholders are the residual owners of the company. So, dividend is only paid when amount is left after making the payment for all other liabilities.

4. **Assertion** (A) The control of the company is not diluted when they go for public deposits.

   Reason (R) The depositors of company are given minor voting rights to keep their preference in consideration.

Ans. (c) In public deposit, the depositors of company are not given any voting rights.

5. **Assertion** (A) Borrowed funds are not considered as permanent source of capital.

   Reason (R) Borrowed funds are raised from external source and are required to be paid back after a stipulated period.

Ans. (a) Both Assertion (A) and Reason (R) are true and Reason (R) is the correct explanation of Assertion (A)

6. **Assertion** (A) To overcome problems during difficult times, a business needs finance.

   Reason (R) During recession and depression, the sales of the business go down and the profitability is adversely affected.

Ans. (a) Both Assertion (A) and Reason (R) are true and Reason (R) is the correct explanation of Assertion (A)

7. **Assertion** (A) Tax benefits are available on dividend paid on preference shares.

   Reason (R) Dividend paid on preference shares is an appropriation of profits.

Ans. (d) Tax benefits are not available on dividend paid on preference shares because of the reason given.

• Case Based MCQs

1. **Direction** *Read the following text and answer the question no. (i) to (vi) on the basis of the same.*

A company is searching options to raise ₹ 20,000 crore from the financial market for diversification and modernisation of existing projects. It hired the services of a renowned financial consultancy firm for suggesting options for the same. The financial consultancy firm suggested a list of options to the board of directors of the company.

It was decided that for the immediate requirement of ₹ 1,500 crore, the company will make a new issue of shares without diluting the right of existing shareholders according to the terms and conditions of the company and ₹ 4,500 crore, would be raised by taking loans from financial institutions.

It was further decided to raise capital to the term of ₹ 6,000 crore through debentures. All these options were accepted by the board of directors. The board further decided that trade credit can be used to finance short-term capital requirements. The company also decided that they will use their undistributed profits in case of shortfall of funds.

   (i) It was decided that for the immediate requirement of ₹ 1,500 crore, the company will make a new issue of shares at a fixed rate of dividend without diluting the control of existing shareholders, according to

the terms and conditions of the company. Name the type of financial securities issued by the company.
(a) Equity shares
(b) Debentures
(c) Commercial papers
(d) Preference shares

Ans. (d) Preference shares

(ii) Which of the following sources of finance used by company does not involve any cost?
(a) Shares
(b) Debentures
(c) Trade credit
(d) Loans from financial institutions

Ans. (c) Trade credit

(iii) Debentures are said to be the economical source of finance because of which of the merits?
(a) Low floatation cost　　(b) Tax benefits
(c) No loss of control　　(d) Fixed interest

Ans. (b) Tax benefits

(iv) ₹ 4,500 crore would be raised by taking loans from financial institutions. Loans from financial institutions are provided for
(a) short-term　　(b) medium-term
(c) long-term　　(d) Both (b) and (c)

Ans. (d) Both (b) and (c)

(v) The board of directors further decided that trade credit can be used to finance short-term capital requirements. Identify one of the sources of trade credit.
(a) Banks　　(b) Traders
(c) Suppliers　　(d) Customers

Ans. (b) Traders

(vi) The usage of undistributed profits indicates the usage of which source of capital?
(a) Bonds　　(b) Equity shares
(c) Preference shares　　(d) None of these

Ans. (d) The undistributed profit indicates retained earnings.

2. Direction *Read the following text and answer the question no. (i) to (vi) on the basis of the same.*

Vinita is the finance manager of Kipla pharma Co. As the company wants to import a piece of new machinery from Japan for its expansion, the capital requirements for the same are estimated to be ₹ 5 crore. Vinita reported that the company is not in a position to bear extra burden of paying interest so the company should use owned capital sources than borrowed capital.

The board of directors are confident about the sales turnover and cash flow position of the company in the coming years and supports the borrowed capital source of raising capital. The company is also considering using retained earnings for the same.

(i) Name the source of owned capital which is available free of cost.
(a) Equity shares　　(b) Preference shares
(c) Retained earnings　　(d) Bonds

Ans. (c) Retained earnings

(ii) Vinita is of the view to finance the fund requirements from owned capital sources rather than from borrowed capital sources as the risk of borrowed capital is …. and cost is …… .
(a) high, low　　(b) low, high
(c) low, low　　(d) high, high

Ans. (a) high, low

(iii) If the cash flow position of the company is strong, the company can raise the required capital by issuing ……… to enjoy tax benefits.
(a) shares
(b) bonds
(c) debentures
(d) commercial papers

Ans. (c) debentures

(iv) The control of shareholders over management will get diluted if the company raises the capital by
(a) equity shares　　(b) debentures
(c) loans　　(d) preference shares

Ans. (a) equity shares

(v) Which of the owned source can be used by company without much of regulations?
(a) Raising share capital
(b) Retained earnings
(c) Using ADR/GDR
(d) Both (b) and (c)

Ans. (b) Retained Earnings

(vi) Which of the following is a merit of retained earnings?
(a) Retained earnings are permanent source of funds for an organisation.
(b) It enhances the capacity of business to absorb unexpected losses.
(c) This source offers a greater degree of operational freedom and flexibility.
(d) All of the above

Ans. (d) All of the above

3. Direction *Read the following text and answer the question no. (i) to (vi) on the basis of the same.*

Sahil Ltd. a firm manufacturing textile, wished to diversify their business. They were considering two options, either to diversify into manufacturing toothpaste or switches. They wanted to invest in the purchase of land, to set up a manufacturing unit in the backward areas of Gujarat. The finance manager of the company was asked by the management to do financial planning by identifying most suitable source of raising long-term funds for financing the investment decisions and short-term sources for working capital decisions.

The objective was to keep the financial risks as low as possible. Therefore, the company decided to source the raw materials using a source of finance which facilitates the purchase of supplies without immediate payment. Moreover, apart from the outside funds used, the company also decided to plough back the profits. The company also decided that after a certain point of time, they will release their IPO and get benefit of the bull run of the market.

(i) Identify which of the following is not the long-term source of finance?

  (a) Equity shares   (b) Retained Earnings

  (c) ADR   (d) Public deposits

Ans. (d) Public deposits

(ii) Name the source of finance having least financial risk on the business.

  (a) Debentures   (b) Trade credit

  (c) Equity shares   (d) Public deposits

Ans (c) Equity shares

(iii) ".... facilitates the purchase of supplies without immediate payment." Identify the source of finance stated above.

  (a) Commercial paper   (b) Retained earnings

  (c) Subsidy   (d) Trade credit

Ans. (d) Trade credit

(iv) Which of the following long-term source of finance is also known as ploughing back of profits?

  (a) Preference shares   (b) Lease financing

  (c) Retained earnings   (d) Equity shares

Ans. (c) Retained earnings

(v) Which of the following factor appears to be the primary factor taken into consideration by the management?

  (a) Cost   (b) Degree of risk

  (c) Financial strength   (d) Tax benefit

Ans. (b) Degree of risk

(vi) Which of these sources of finance would be raised through IPO as stated in the last line of the text?

  (a) Preference shares   (b) Lease financing

  (c) Retained earnings   (d) Equity shares

Ans. (d) Equity shares

PART 2

Subjective Questions

● Short Answer (SA) Type Questions

1. Why is finance important for business?

Ans. Finance is the life blood of the business. Funds are required to commence and carry on business. All business activities such as planning, organising, managing, controlling, purchasing, selling, directing, marketing, etc cannot take place without finance. Business needs funds for purchasing fixed and current assets, for day-to-day operations, purchase of raw material, to pay salaries, etc.

2. For the successful running of a business, it is necessary to determine the amount of working capital. Do you agree? If yes, then give reasons in support of your answer.

Ans. Yes, I agree with the statement. Working capital is that portion of capital which is used to conduct day-to-day operations. It is very important for a business to determine the required amount of working capital.

The reasons for estimating required working capital are

  (i) Prosperity and progress of the projects can be maintained by adequate working capital.

  (ii) Adequate working capital enables a firm to improve the efficiency and profitability of its operations.

  (iii) It is also required to channelise the day-to-day operations. That's why it is also called circulating or revolving capital.

3. Komalika wants to start her own business dealing in high end crockery items. She decides to arrange for initial finance from her savings. However, her savings are not enough to fulfil all the initial needs of the business. She seeks help of her husband, who works in government sector.

He advises her that to start her business with limited finance and then use the revenues earned by the business to fulfil other financial requirements. Is the view of Komalika's husband justified? Why or why not?

Ans. No, I don't think that the view of Komalika's husband is justified. Adequate finance is required in the business because of following reasons

  (i) **Necessary to Start Business** Every new venture needs money to buy plant and machinery or to conduct certain activities. All financial needs will not be estimated in the absence of this concept.

  (ii) **Necessary for Business Cycle** No matter how well the business is doing, a good finance manager has to prepare for rainy or even for stormy season. Business and economic cycles bring dark clouds that one can't predict. That's why financial plans are created for downturns.

  (iii) **Necessary for Growth** Success can bring a business to a difficult crossroads. Sometimes in order to attain more or to achieve greater success, a company needs significant financial investment to acquire new capital, staff or inventory. This can only be possible after proper arrangements of business finance.

4. What are the different expenditures that any firm incurs in

  (i) Short-term   (ii) Medium-term

  (iii) Long-term

Ans. (i) Short-term

    (a) Purchase of raw material.

    (b) Payment of telephone bill, electricity bill, etc.

  (ii) Medium-term

    (a) Expenditure made on renovation of office.

    (b) Expenditure made on the promotion of company's product.

  (iii) Long-term

    (a) Purchase of building

    (b) Purchase of machinery

5. Differentiate between owner's funds and borrowed funds on the basis of

  (i) Reward

  (ii) Security

  (iii) Order of payment

Ans. Difference between owner's funds and borrowed funds.

Basis	Owner's Funds	Borrowed Funds
Reward	Owner's funds earn rewards in the form of share in profit, as in the form of dividend.	Borrowed funds earn rewards in the form of interest.
Security	These funds are raised without providing for security of assets.	These funds are raised on security of assets.
Order of Payment	They rank last in the order of payment.	They have priority in the order of payment.

6. Sun Rise company issues 10,000 shares of ₹ 10 each for a total value of ₹ 1,00,000. With reference to the given statement, explain the meaning of the term share, share capital and shareholders.

Ans. **Shares** The capital of a company is divided into small units and each such unit is referred to as a 'share'. Each share forms a unit of ownership and is offered for sale to raise the capital of the company. Shares are classified as equity shares and preference shares.

Share Capital Total amount raised by issue of shares constitute the share capital of the company.

Shareholders The persons who buy shares are referred to as 'shareholders'.

In the given example, number of shares issued are 10,000, share capital is of ₹ 1,00,000 and the persons who purchase these shares are the shareholders.

7. Discuss the features of equity shares as a source of finance.

Ans. Features of equity shares are

  (i) The equity shareholders are the primary risk bearers as they provide fixed capital to the business.

  (ii) The equity share capital is not redeemable during the lifetime of the company.

  (iii) Returns are uncertain as the rate of dividend is not fixed.

  (iv) Equity shareholders can participate in the company's decisions and management.

8. Preference shareholders have some preferential rights in the capital structure of any company. Comment.

Ans. The following preferential rights are enjoyed by preference shareholders

  (i) Receiving a fixed rate of dividend, out of the net profits of the company, before any dividend is declared for equity shareholders.

  (ii) Preference over equity shareholders in receiving their capital after the claims of the company's creditors have been settled but before any amount is paid to equity shareholders at the time of liquidation.

9. Preference shares are not suitable for those investors who are willing to take risk and are interested in higher returns. This highlights one of the demerits of preference shares. State any other four demerits of preference shares.

Ans. Demerits of preference shares are

  (i) These shares dilute the claim of equity shareholders over the assets of the company.

  (ii) The company has to pay higher rates of dividends to the preference shareholders as compared to interest on debentures.

  (iii) The dividend on these shares is to be paid only when the company earns profit. Thus, the returns are not assured and they are unable to attract the investors.

  (iv) The dividend paid on preference shares is not deductible from profits as expense. Thus, there is no tax savings, as in the case of interest on loans.

10. Shares are used to raise funds by the company. However, there is a distinction in shares. There are two types of shares – preference and equity. Differentiate between equity shares and preference shares on any three basis.

Ans. The differences between equity shares and preference shares are (any three)

Basis	Equity Shares	Preference Shares
Participation in Management	Full right to participate.	No right to participate.
Sequence of Dividend	Dividend is paid last of all.	Preference is given in payment of dividend.
Sequence of Refund of Capital	On winding up of the company, capital is refunded after preference shares.	Preference is given in refunding the capital.
Refund of Capital During Lifetime	Not possible at all.	Capital can be refunded in case of redeemable preference shares.
Permanency of Dividend	Dividend is uncertain as it fluctuates with the amount of divisible profits decision of board of directors.	Dividend is certain and fixed.

11. Amar owns a small farm in which he grows flowers. He is able to earn a small amount of profit, but being of an ambitious nature, he wants to take over a neighbouring farm and increase the range of flowers he is selling.

He is of the view that he will need long-term finance for this purpose and plans to take a bank loan to pay for the take-over. He has already borrowed money to buy a new tractor.

On the basis of above case, answer the following questions.

(i) What is meant by 'long-term sources of finance'?

(ii) Identify and explain a form of internal finance Amar could have used to buy the tractor.

(iii) What factors would the bank consider before granting loan to Amar?

Ans. (i) Long-term sources of finance means those sources which provide finance to business firms for a period exceeding five years.

(ii) A form of internal finance which Amar could have used to buy the tractor is 'retained earnings'. These earnings are a part of trading profits which are not withdrawn by the proprietor, but are reinvested by them in the business.

(iii) The bank would consider the following factors before granting loan to Amar
   (a) Amount of loan required.
   (b) Period for which the loan is required.
   (c) Security offered.
   (d) Profit earning capacity of the business
   (e) Repayment schedule of any previous loan taken.

12. Though retained earnings are firm's own source of funding and they are free to use them but using retained earnings can sometimes prove to be disadvantageous. Do you agree? Explain.

Ans. Yes, I agree that using retained earnings can sometimes prove to be disadvantageous. Following points helps in explaining the demerits of retained earnings

(i) Excessive ploughing back may cause dissatisfaction amongst the shareholders, as they would get lower dividends.

(ii) As the profits of business are fluctuating, it is an uncertain source of fund.

(iii) Firms do not recognise the opportunity cost associated with this source, leading to sub-optimal use of funds.

13. What is the difference between GDR and ADR?

(NCERT)

Ans.

Basis	GDR	ADR
Location of Financial Markets	Global Depository Receipts (GDR) can be bought and sold in many international markets.	American Depository Receipts (ADR) can be bought and sold only in America.
Disclosure Requirements	Issue of GDRs do not require strict disclosure requirements.	Issue of ADRs require strict disclosure requirements.
Liquidity	GDRs are less liquid.	ADRs are more liquid.
Maintenance Costs	Maintenance costs of GDRs are less than that of ADRs.	Maintenance costs of ADRs are more than that of GDRs.

14. A seminar was held in New York on the problems generally classified into owners fund and borrowed funds. ABC Ltd. can raise required funds by employing both the above mentioned sources to fulfill its needs of finance.

Its topic was "The difference finance sources available at the global level in the modern context". 200 representatives from different countries participated in this seminar. All the representatives expressed their respective opinions.

One of the sources of finance discussed in the seminar was such through which the foreign companies could issue their securities in India. Looking at the great possibilities of obtaining capital from the investors in India, all of them showed a great interest in the discussion of the source.

Another source of finance which created interest in everyone was the source through which money could be obtained from the investors in America and other European countries. Since this source was concerned with a very big area, the number of people who took interest in its was also large. One of the Indian representatives throw light on the special characteristics of this source. You are required to identify the source discussed by highlighting the relevant lines.

Ans. (i) Indian Depository Receipts (IDR)
Line "One of the sources of finance .... securities in India."
(ii) Global Depository Receipts (GDR)
Line "Another source .... European countries".
(iii) American Depository Receipts (ADR)
Line "In the final session ... ... only in America."

15. Mahindra and Mahindra was the first company in India to issue convertible zero interest debentures in January 1990. Recently, the board of Titan Industries has approved the issue of partly convertible debentures on a right's basis to raise around ₹ 126.83 crore. The issue will comprise 21 lakh partly convertible debentures of ₹ 600 each in the ratio of one partly convertible debenture for every 20 equity shares held in the company to the shareholders.
On the basis of above case, answer the following questions
(i) Explain the meaning of convertible zero interest debentures issued by Mahindra and Mahindra.
(ii) Explain the meaning of partly convertible debentures on right's basis. **(NCERT)**

Ans. (i) Convertible zero interest debentures are debentures which carry no interest and are convertible into equity shares at the end of a specified period.
(ii) Partly convertible debentures on right's basis means that a part of these debentures will be converted into equity shares at the end of the stipulated period and that these debentures can be subscribed by only existing equity shareholders of the company.

16. What advantages does issue of debentures provide over the issue of equity shares?

Ans. Following are the advantages of issuing debentures instead of equity shares
(i) Debentures are fixed charge funds and do not participate in the profits of the company.
(ii) Financing through debentures does not dilute control of shareholders on management as debentures do not carry voting rights.
(iii) Financing through debentures is less costly as compared to cost of equity capital as the interest payment on debentures is tax deductible.

17. State the demerits of public deposits.

Ans. Demerits of public deposits are
(i) New companies generally find it difficult to raise funds through public deposits due to lack of goodwill.
(ii) It is an unreliable source of finance as the public may not always respond when the company needs money.
(iii) Collection of public deposits may prove difficult, particularly when the size of deposits required is large.

18. The company getting finance through public deposits enjoys some benefits. Explain.

Ans. Following points illustrate the benefits of public deposits to the company
(i) The procedure of obtaining deposits is simple and does not contain restrictive conditions.
(ii) Cost of public deposits is generally lower than the cost of borrowings from banks and others institutions.
(iii) Public deposits do not usually create any charge on the assets of the company.
(iv) As the depositors do not have voting rights, the control of the company is not diluted.

19. Along with financial assistance, financial institutions also provide technical assistance and managerial services to business units. This reflects one of the merits of obtaining finance through financial institutions. Write any three more such merits.

Ans. Merits of obtaining finance from financial institutions are as follows
(i) Financial institutions provide long-term finance, which is not provided by the commercial banks.
(ii) A financial institution, before extending financial support to a business unit, conducts detailed study about its state of affairs. Only a promising and sound business is able to get a loan from these institutions. So, if a firm gets a loan from these institutes, then this will also help in raising the goodwill of the borrowing company in the capital market.
(iii) Repayment can be made in easy instalments therefore; it does not prove to be a burden on the business.

20. State the disadvantages of financial institutions as a source of finance.

Ans. Disadvantages of financial institutions as a source of finance are as follows
(i) Too many formalities are required by these institutes to grant a loan.
(ii) Restrictions are imposed by these institutes on companies such as restrictions on the payment of dividends or restrictions on the autonomy of management.
(iii) Generally, the financial institutions have their nominees in the Board of Directors of the borrowed company. This restricts their powers and the borrowed companies feel helpless in certain cases.

21. Mr. Anil Singh has been running a restaurant for the last two years. The excellent quality of food has made the restaurant popular in no time. Motivated by the success of his business, Mr. Singh is now contemplating the idea of opening a chain of similar restaurants at different places.

However, the money available with him from his personal sources is not sufficient to meet the expansion requirements of his business.

His father told him that he can enter into a partnership with the owner of another restaurant, who will bring in more funds, but it would also require sharing of profits and control of business.

He is also thinking of taking a bank loan. As a financial consultant, state the various sources of owned funds and debt funds that Anil Singh can use.

(NCERT)

Ans. The various sources of owned funds that Anil Singh can use are

  (i) Selling a part of his business to other partners.

  (ii) Issuing equity shares and preference shares (if he decides to form a joint stock company).

The various sources of debt funds are (any two)

  (i) Loan from commercial banks.

  (ii) Loan from specialised financial institutions.

  (iii) Issue of debentures (if he decides to form a joint stock company).

• Long Answer (LA) Type Questions

1. State any three merits and three limitations of equity shares.

Ans. Merits of equity shares are (Any three)

  (i) Equity shares are suitable for those investors who are willing to assume risk for higher returns.

  (ii) Payment of dividend to the equity shareholders is not compulsory. Therefore, there is no burden on the company.

  (iii) It is considered as a good source of long-term finance. A company is not required to pay back the equity capital during its lifetime. It is repaid only at the time of liquidation of company. Also, since it is paid in last, even on liquidation, therefore it provides a cushion for creditors. Thus, it is a permanent source of capital.

  (iv) Funds can be raised through equity shares without creating any charge on the assets of the company. These assets can be mortgaged to raise finance from other sources.

Demerits of equity shares are as follows (Any three)

  (i) Investors who want steady income may not prefer equity shares due to fluctuating returns.

  (ii) The cost of equity shares is more as compared to other sources of funds.

  (iii) Every successive issue of equity shares dilutes the voting power and earnings of existing equity shareholders.

  (iv) Many formalities and procedural delays are involved while raising funds through equity.

2. Rohit Ltd. is a manufacturing firm which has been running in deep losses due to the onset of pandemic. The company wants to innovate the products to increase the sales and have therefore decided to purchase a new machinery for the same. The company decided to use its funds which it has saved over the years to fund this machinery. Which source of finance is highlighted here? Define. Also, give the merits of the same.

Ans. The source of finance highlighted here is 'retained earnings'. It means that part of trading profits which are not distributed in the form of dividends, but retained by directors for future expansion of the company. This is also referred to as 'ploughing back of profits'.

Merits of retained earnings are

  (i) Retained earnings are a permanent source of funds for an organisation.

  (ii) Retained earnings do not involve any explicit cost in the form of interest, dividend or floatation cost.

  (iii) This source offers a greater degree of operational freedom and flexibility.

  (iv) It enhances the capacity of business to absorb unexpected losses.

3. Debenture issued by a company is an acknowledgment that the company has borrowed a certain amount of money, which it promises to repay at a future date. However, there are both merits and demerits of debentures. Explain those merits and demerits.

Ans. Merits of debentures are (any three)

  (i) It is preferred by investors who want fixed income at lesser risk.

  (ii) Debentures are fixed charge funds and do not participate in profits of the company.

  (iii) The issue of debentures is suitable in the situation when the sales and earnings are relatively stable.

  (iv) Financing through debentures does not dilute control of equity shareholders on management.

  (v) Financing through debentures is less costly as compared to cost of preference or equity capital.

Limitations of debentures are

  (i) As fixed charge instruments, debentures put a permanent burden on the earnings of a company.

  (ii) In case of redeemable debentures, the company has to make provisions for repayment on the specified date.

  (iii) With the issue of debentures, the capacity of a company to further borrow funds reduces.

4. Differentiate between shares and debentures on the basis of

(i) Nature of finance   (ii) Nature and rate of return
(iii) Status of holders   (iv) Degree of control
(v) Security offered   (vi) Level of risk

Ans. The differences between shares and debentures are

Basis	Shares	Debentures
Nature of Finance	Shares are a part of owner's fund.	Debentures are a part of debt fund.
Nature and Rate of Return	Dividend is the return on shares. The rate of dividend is not fixed and is dependent on the profits of the company and the decision of the management.	Interest is the return on debentures. The rate of interest is fixed and is required to be paid even if the company incurs losses.
Status of Holders	Shareholders are deemed to be the owners of the company.	Debenture holders are deemed to be the creditors of the company.
Degree of Control	Shareholders can exercise reasonable degree of control on the affairs of the business by exercising their right to vote.	Debenture holders are in no position to control the affairs of the business as they do not have the right to vote.
Security Offered	No security is required to be offered at the time of issue of shares.	Security is required to be offered, either by creating a charge on assets or by mortgaging the assets, at the time of issue of debentures.
Level of Risk	Shareholders assume a high level of risk.	Risk is comparatively lower for debenture holders.

5. Write a short note on the following three financial institutions

(i) Industrial Finance Corporation of India (IFCI)
(ii) State Financial Corporations (SFCs)
(iii) Life Insurance Corporation of India (LIC)

Ans. (i) **Industrial Finance Corporation of India** (IFCI) It was established in July, 1948 as a statutory corporation under the Industrial Finance Corporation Act, 1948.

Its objectives include assistance towards balanced regional development and encouraging new entrepreneurs to enter into the priority sectors of the economy. IFCI has also contributed to the development of management education in the country.

(ii) **State Financial Corporations** (SFCs) They are established by the state governments under the State Financial Corporations Act, 1951 for providing medium and short-term finance to industries which are outside the scope of the IFCI. Its scope is wider

than IFCI as it covers not only public limited companies, but also private limited companies, partnership firms and proprietary concerns.

(iii) **Life Insurance Corporation of India** (LIC) It was set up in 1956 under the LIC Act, 1956 after nationalising 245 existing insurance companies. It mobilises savings in the form of insurance premium and makes it available to industrial concerns in the form of direct loans and underwriting and subscribing to shares and debentures.

6. Commercial banks accept deposits from general public and extend loans to those who are in need. This also includes companies who are in need of capital for multiple business purposes. Getting finance from commercial banks has some merits and some limitations, explain.

Ans. Merits of loan from commercial banks are

(i) Banks provide timely assistance to business by providing funds as and when needed by it.
(ii) Secrecy of business can be maintained as the information supplied to the bank by the borrowers is kept confidential.
(iii) Formalities such as issue of prospectus and underwriting are not required for raising loans from a bank.
(iv) Loan from a bank is a flexible source of finance as the loan amount can be increased according to business needs

Limitations of loan from commercial banks are

(i) Funds are generally available for short periods.
(ii) Banks make detailed investigation of the company's affairs, financial structure etc., and may also ask for security of assets and personal sureties.
(iii) In some cases, difficult terms and conditions are imposed by banks for the grant of loan.

7. Sujeet is a proprietor of a stationery trading firm. The business of the firm is flourishing over last 18 months. Sujeet decided to expand the product line and include basic confectionery items as well. He negotiated deals with multiple suppliers and stroked contracts in such a way that he facilitated the purchase of supplies without immediate payments.

Which source of finance is highlighted here? Also, explain the concept of the same and write three merits and demerits each.

Ans. The source of finance highlighted here is 'trade credit'. Trade credit facilitates the purchase of supplies without immediate payment.

Such credit appears in the records of the buyer as sundry creditors or accounts payable. It is commonly used by business organisation as a source of short-term financing. It is granted to those customers who have reasonable amount of financial standing and goodwill.

Merits of trade credit are

(i) Trade credit is a convenient and continuous source of funds.

(ii) It may be readily available in case the credit worthiness of the customers is known to the seller.

(iii) It helps to promote the sale of an organisation.

Demerits of trade credit are

(i) This may motivate a firm to overtrade.

(ii) Only limited amount of funds can be raised through this source.

(iii) It is generally a costly source of fund as compared to others, as sellers charge more for goods sold on credit.

8. X-cellent company is well established domestically. It manufactures educative toys for children. The company has recently analysed the prospects of going global and founds them to be very promising. Now, it wants to choose suitable funds to finance the proposition.

State some of the factors which should be considered by X-cellent company, before making a choice for source of funds.

Ans. Following points should be considered to make a choice for source of funds

(i) **Cost** Two types of costs are there viz. the cost of procurement and the cost of utilising the funds. These two costs should be considered very carefully before making a choice.

(ii) **Financial Strength** The financial strength of an enterprise is also a key determinant in making the choice of funds. If the firm is financially strong with a steady flow of income, then it can raise finance by issuing debt instruments. Otherwise, owner's funds would be the logical choice.

(iii) **Form of Organisation** The form of organisation also influences the decision of a finance manager while deciding about the source of finance.

As we are aware that there are various forms of business organisations such as sole proprietorship, partnership, joint stock company, etc. A joint stock company can raise funds from various sources, but on the other side a sole proprietor has access to limited sources to raise funds.

(iv) **Control** It is also an important factor to be considered while raising finance. If the existing owners do not want to dilute their control on the business, then they should opt for debt funds, otherwise they can raise finance from owner's funds.

(v) **Degree of Risk** The risk associated with each of the source is different. Thus, a finance manager must evaluate the degree of risk involved in each source to make an appropriate choice.

(vi) **Tax Benefit** To avail tax benefits, companies consider every possible source very minutely. They should remember that interest paid on debt funds would be admissible as business expense and will generate tax benefits, but dividend paid will not give any such benefit to the firm.

Chapter Test

Multiple Choice Questions

1. Which of the following can be the negative implications of non-payment of debts?
 (a) Higher interest costs   (b) Loss of goodwill
 (c) Fines and penalties   (d) All of these

2. The return earned by .... is known as interest.
 (a) equity shareholders   (b) preference shareholders
 (c) debenture holders   (d) Both (b) and (c)

3. Equity shareholders are also called .... of company.
 (a) borrowers   (b) partners
 (c) owners   (d) Both (b) and (c)

4. **Statement I** Public deposits are not issued against security of assets of the company.
Statement II FCCBs are issued in foreign currency.
Alternatives
 (a) Statement I is correct and statement II is wrong   (b) Statement II is correct and Statement I is wrong
 (c) Both the statements are correct   (d) Both the statements are incorrect

5. **Statement I** Public deposits are issued in foreign currency.
Statement II Debentures create charge on assets of the company.
Alternatives
 (a) Statement I is correct and statement II is wrong   (b) Statement II is correct and Statement I is wrong
 (c) Both the statements are correct   (d) Both the statements are incorrect

Short Answer (SA) Type Questions

1. What do you mean by fixed capital? What type of organisation need more fixed capital?

2. Mridul is an ambitious man. He wants to participate in the affairs of the company. What will he choose amongst the two— preference share or equity share? Also, give reason for the same.

3. Devika is considering taking loan from a commercial bank for her business. Advise her on the same by highlighting the cons of borrowing from commercial bank.

4. "Umya manufacturers" is a firm manufacturing cricket balls in India. The company had been fairly successful in last many years. The owners of the firm decided to raise finance from public and launched its IPO. The company received positive feedback from the market and used the IPO proceeds to expand its manufacturing to pink cricket balls as well. The company earned lot of profits in the following year. Instead of distributing entire profits to the owners in the form of dividend, some profits were re-invested in business in order to finance the future earnings of the business.
 (i) Identify the source of finance discussed in the last part of the passage.
 (ii) Highlight the demerits of the given method.

5. Name and explain any four reasons as to why businesses require finance.

Long Answer (LA) Type Questions

1. Burman Ltd. is a medicines trading firm. The family owning the business has got some ancestral land vacant in the recent times. The company decides to make use of this land and expand its product line. Consequently, it started to trade the medical equipments as well. The company needed to purchase raw materials, payment of electricity bill, rent, etc.
 (i) Identify and define the type of business finance needed by the company. Also, what type of source of finance is required for the same?
 (ii) On what factors, these requirements are dependent upon?

2. Differentiate between owner's fund and borrower's fund on the basis of
 (i) Meaning   (ii) Nature   (iii) Risk   (iv) Control
 (v) Nature of obligation   (vi) Rate of return

Answers

Multiple Choice Questions

1. (d)   *2. (c)*   *3. (c)*   *4. (c)*   *5. (b)*

For Detailed Solutions
Scan the code

CHAPTER 2

Small Business and Entrepreneurship Development

In this Chapter...

- Entrepreneurship Development
- Startup India Scheme
- Intellectual Property Rights (IPR)
- Small Scale Enterprises
- Government Assistance to Small Business Units

Entrepreneurship Development

Entrepreneurship development refers to the process of enhancing entrepreneurial skills and knowledge through structured training and institution-building programmes.

The whole point of entrepreneurship development is to increase the number of entrepreneurs. Entrepreneur creates an enterprise through the process called entrepreneurship.

Entrepreneurship is the process of setting up one's own business as distinct from pursuing any other economic activity, be it employment or practising some profession.

Entrepreneur is the person who set-up an enterprise, take the risks, accumulates all the resources required to carry out production or perform services and creates an innovative product or service.

Enterprise The output of the process, i.e., the business unit is called an enterprise.

Characteristics of Entrepreneurship

1. **Systematic Activity** Entrepreneurship has certain temperamental, skill and other knowledge and competency requirements that can be acquired, learnt and developed, both by formal educational and vocational training as well as by observation and work experience.

2. **Lawful and Purposeful Activity** The object of entrepreneurship is lawful business. It is important to take note that one may try to legitimise unlawful actions as entrepreneurship on the grounds that just as entrepreneurship entails risk, so does illicit businesses.

3. **Innovation** Entrepreneurship is creative in the sense that it involves innovation, introduction of new products, discovery of new markets and sources of supply of inputs, technological breakthroughs as well as introduction of newer organisational forms for doing things better, cheaper, faster and, in the present context, in a manner that causes the least harm to the ecology/ environment.

4. **Organisation of Production** Entrepreneur, in response to a perceived business opportunity, mobilises the resources into a productive enterprise or firm. In an economy with a well-developed financial system, he has to convince just the funding institutions and with the capital so arranged he may enter into contracts of supply of equipment, materials, utilities (such as water and electricity) and technology.

5. **Risk-taking** Entrepreneurship involves risk as individuals opting for a career in entrepreneurship take a bigger risk that is involved in a career in employment or practice of a profession as there is no 'assured' payoff. However, entrepreneurs are so sure of their capabilities that they can convert situations with higher risks into opportunities.

Need of Entrepreneurship Development

1. **Employment Opportunities** It enables entrepreneurs to create more/additional employment opportunities for youth.
2. **Economic Independence** Entrepreneurs develop substituted products of imported goods and prevent the over-dependence on the other countries.
3. **Capital Formation** It encourage the establishment of new industries in economy leading to capital formation in country.
4. **Development of Backward and Tribal Areas** It leads to scattering of economic activities in all areas of the country.
5. **More Utilisation of Natural Resources** It enables the economy to utilise and explore the abundant of natural resources.
6. **Economic Growth and Development** It provides the base of industrialisation leading to economic growth and development.

Entrepreneurship Development Process

It is a process meant to develop entrepreneurial abilities among entrepreneurs. It is a process to

- enhance the motivation, knowledge and skills of potential entrepreneurs.
- reforming the entrepreneurial behaviour.
- assist entrepreneurs to develop their own ventures.

Startup India Scheme

The Startup India Scheme is a flagship initiative of the Government of India with an objective to carve a strong ecosystem for nurturing innovation and startups in the country.

The Government of India aims to empower startups to grow through innovation and design. The scheme specifically aims to

- trigger an entrepreneurial culture, inculcate entrepreneurial values in the society at large and influence the mindset of people towards entrepreneurship.
- create awareness about the charms of being an entrepreneur and the process of entrepreneurship, especially among the youth.
- encourage more dynamic startups by motivating enducated youth, scientists and technologists to consider entrepreneurship as a lucrative, preferred and viable career.
- support the early phase of entrepreneurship development, including the pre-startup, nascent, as well as, early post startup phase and growth enterprises.
- broad base the entrepreneurial supply by meeting specific needs of under-represented target groups, like women, socially and economically backward communities, scheduled castes and scheduled tribes; under represented regions to achieve inclusiveness and sustainable development to address the needs of the population at the bottom of the pyramid.

Startup India Initiative Action Points

1. **Simplification and Handholding** Friendly and flexible, simplifications are announced.
2. **Startup India Hub** It is a single point of contact for the entire startup ecosystem to enable knowledge exchange and funding access.
3. **Legal Support and Fast-tracking Patent Examination** The scheme for Startups Intellectual Property Protections (SIPP) is envisaged to facilitate protection of patents of innovative startups.
4. **Easy Exit** In the event of a business failure and wind up of operations, procedures are being adopted to reallocate capital and resources towards more productive avenues.
5. **Harnessing Private Sector for Incubator Setup** The government envisages setting up of incubators across the country in PPP mode.
6. **Tax Exemption** The profits of startup initiatives are exempted for income tax for a period of three years.

Ways to Fund Startup

1. **Bootstrapping** It is considered as the first funding option which involves entrepreneur's personal savings and resources.
2. **Crowd Funding** It is the pooling of resources by a group of people for a common goal.
3. **Angel Investment** Angel investors are individuals with surplus cash who offer capital and even offer mentoring or advice.
4. **Venture Capital** There are professionally managed funds which are invested in companies that have huge potential. Venture capitalists also provide expertise and mentorship.
5. **Incubators** They provide professional services that facilitates the development of new business by providing resources, support and advice. e.g.,
     (i) Innovation and Entrepreneurship (SINE), IIT Mumbai.
     (ii) Technology Business Incubator, IIT Delhi.
6. **Accelerators** These are organisations that offer a range of support service and funding opportunities for startups. e.g.,
     (i) Amity Innovation Incubator
     (ii) IAN Business Incubator, Kyron
7. **Micro Finance and NBFCs** Micro finance is basically access to financial services to those who either do not have access to conventional banking services or have not qualified for a bank loan.

   NBFCs (Non-Banking Financial Corporation) provides banking services without meeting legal requirement/definition of a bank.

Intellectual Property Rights (IPR)

"Intellectual Property (IP) is defined as the creation of the mind, inventions, literary and artistic works and symbol name, images and designs used in commerce."

— World Intellectual Property Organisation (WIPO)

Importance of IPRs

- Exclusive right on the use of IP is the biggest motivation behind creation of intellectual property.
- Customers get improved goods and services due to IPR.
- Entrepreneurs are enabled to earn more revenue due to IPR.
- It is cost saving mechanism for society through effectively utilisation of resources.

Types of IPRs

1. **Copyright** It is a legal right created by the law that grant the creator of an original work's exclusive rights for its use and distribution. Following works are protected under copyright
   - Original literary, dramatic, musical or artistic works.
   - Sound recording, films and broadcasts.
   - Typographical arrangements of published editions.

2. **Trademark** It provides recognisable sign, design or expression which identifies products or services of a particular source from those of others. e.g., McDonald's double arches, Apple computer's, Apple sign of Android.

3. **Geographical Indication** It is primarily an indication which identifies agricultural, natural or manufactured products (handicrafts, industrial goods and food stuffs) originating from a definite geographical territory, where a given quality, reputation or other characteristic are essentially attributable to its geographical origin.

   GIs are part of our collective and intellectual heritage that needs to be protected and promoted.

   Goods protected and registered as GI are categorised into agricultural products, natural, handicrafts, manufactured goods and food stuffs.

   GI represents collective goodwill of a geographical region, which has built itself over centuries.

4. **Patent** Patent is an exclusive right granted in respect of an invention which may be product or process that provides a new and inventive way of doing something. The examples of patents are telephone radio, optical fibre, i-pod and ballpoint pens.

5. **Design** A 'design' includes shape, pattern and arrangement of lines or colour combination that is applied to any article. It is a protection given to aesthetic appearance or eye-catching features. The term of protection of a design is valid for 10 years, which can be renewed for further 5 years after expiration of this term, during which a registered design can only be used after getting a license from its owner and once the validity period is over, the design is in public domain.

6. **Plant Variety** It is essentially grouping plants into categories based on their botanical characteristics. It is a type of variety which is bred and developed by farmers. This helps in conserving, improving and making available plant genetic resources. e.g. hybrid versions of potatoes, etc. Such protection promotes investment in R&D, recognises Indian farmers as cultivators, conservers and breeders as well as facilitates high quality seeds and planting material. This leads to the growth of the seed industry.

7. **Semiconductor Integrated Circuits Layout Design** A semiconductor is an integral part of every computer chip. A semiconductor layout design means a layout of transistors and other circuitry elements used and formed on a semiconductor material, as an insulating material or inside the semiconductor material. Its design is to perform an electronic circuitry function.

8. **Trade Secret** It is a information that is not generally known to public and confers economic benefit. It is the subject of reasonable efforts by the holder to maintain its secrecy. e.g. CoCa Cola's recipe is a trade secret. Trade secrets are protected without any procedural formalities for an unlimited period.

IP and Business

Protecting and managing the intellectual property is the most crucial thing for any business enterprise. In order to remain ahead of the competitors, every business has to continuously innovate.

Moreover, every business enterprise must respect others' IP, not only on ethical grounds, but also legal. Intellectual rights can be critical in aiding new ventures monetise their ideas and establish competitiveness in the market by extending the protective umbrella offered by IPRs.

Small Scale Enterprises

Small scale enterprises are defined in terms of their size. The size of an enterprise depends on a number of parameters such as number of persons employed in business, capital invested in business, volume of output, power consumed, etc.

Micro, Small and Medium Enterprises Development (MSMED) Act, 2006 defines small enterprises in the following manner

For Industrial/Manufacturing Enterprises

1. **Micro Enterprise** In micro enterprise, the investment in plant and machinery does not exceed ₹ 25 lakh.

2. **Small Enterprise** In small enterprise, the investment in plant and machinery is more than ₹ 25 lakh but does not exceed ₹ 5 crore.

3. **Medium Enterprise** In medium enterprise, the investment in plant and machinery is more than ₹ 5 crore but does not exceed ₹ 10 crore.

For Service Enterprises

1. **Micro Enterprise** In micro enterprise, the investment in equipment does not exceed ₹ 10 lakh.

2. **Small Enterprise** In small enterprise, the investment in equipment is more than ₹ 10 lakh but does not exceed ₹ 2 crore.

3. **Medium Enterprise** In medium enterprise, the investment in equipment is more than ₹ 2 crore but does not exceed ₹ 5 crore.

Some Other Types of Small Scale Enterprises

1. **Village Industries** Village industry has been defined as any industry located in a rural area which produces any goods, renders any service with or without the use of power and in which the fixed capital investment per head or artisan or worker is specified by the central government, from time to time.

2. **Cottage Industries** Cottage industries are also known as rural industries or traditional industries. They are not defined by capital investment criteria as in the case of other small scale industries. However, cottage industries are characterised by certain features like

   - These are organised by individuals, with private resources.
   - They normally use family labour and locally available talent.
   - The equipment used is simple. Capital investment is small.
   - They produce simple products, normally in their own premises.
   - They use indigenous technology for production of goods.

Role of Small Scale Industries (SSI) in India

1. **Contribution in GDP** Small industries contribute almost 40% of the gross industrial value added and 45% of the total exports (direct and indirect) from India.

2. **Employment Generation** In India, small industries are the second largest employers of human resources, after agriculture.

3. **Supply Variety of Products** Small industries in our country supply enormous variety of products which include goods of mass consumption such as readymade garments, hosiery goods, stationery items, soaps and detergents, domestic utensils, etc.

4. **Balanced Regional Development** These industries can be opened anywhere in the country, without any locational constraints and the benefits of industrialisation can be reaped by every region.

5. **Provide Business Opportunities** The skills and talents of people can be channelled into business ideas, which can be converted into reality with little or nil capital investment.

6. **Low Cost of Production** They also enjoy the advantage of low cost of production due to minimum establishment and running costs.

7. **Quick Decisions** Due to the small size of the organisation, quick and timely decisions can be taken without consulting many people.

8. **Customised Production** They are best suited for customised production i.e., designing the product as per the tastes/ preferences/needs of an individual.

9. **Maintain Good Personal Relations** Small industries have the inherent strength of adaptability and have personal touch with both customers and employees.

Role of Small Scale Industries in Rural India

1. **Non-farm Employment** Rural households have varied and multiple sources of income and participate in a wide range of non-agricultural activities due to setting up of agro-based rural small industries.

2. **Employment for Artisans** Cottage and rural industries play an important role in providing employment opportunities in the rural areas.

3. **Prevention of Migration** Development of rural and village industries can also prevent migration of rural population to urban areas in search of employment.

4. **Poverty Alleviation** Small industries are significant absorbers of surplus labour, thereby addressing the problems of poverty and unemployment.

5. **Socio-economic Aspects** These industries contribute towards socio-economic aspects such as reduction in income inequalities, etc.

Problems of Small Business

Small scale industries are at a distinct disadvantage as compared to large scale industries. Following are the major problems that are faced by small business

1. **Finance** One of the severe problems faced by SSIs is the non-availability of adequate finance to carry out its operations. These units lack in credit worthiness and have a small capital base. As a result, they heavily depend on local financial resources and frequently become the victims of exploitation by the money lenders.

   Due to delayed payment from customers and locking up of their capital in unsold stocks, small units suffer from lack of adequate working capital. Banks also do not provide funds to them.

2. **Raw Materials** If the required materials are not available, small businesses have to compromise on the

quality or have to pay high price to get good quality materials. Their bargaining power is relatively low due to the small quantity of purchases made by them.

They cannot afford to buy in bulk because they do not have the facility to store material and neither do they have the necessary finance.

3. **Managerial Skills** Small business is generally promoted and operated by a single person, who may not possess technical and managerial skills to run the business.

4. **Labour** Due to low remuneration, talented people are not attracted to work with small business, firms as they cannot afford to pay higher salaries to the employees this affects employee willingness to work hard and produce more. Thus, productivity per employee is relatively low and employee turnover is generally high.

5. **Marketing** Small scale enterprises are unable to meet the expenses of marketing activities. They depend on middlemen who exploit them by paying low prices for their goods and delaying their payments.

6. **Quality** Many small business organisations do not adhere to desired standards of quality. Instead, they concentrate on cutting the cost and keeping the prices low. As they do not maintain quality, they are not able to compete in global markets.

7. **Capacity Utilisation** Due to lack of marketing skills leading to lack of demand, many small business firms have to operate below full capacity due to which their operating costs tend to increase. This leads to sickness and closure of the business.

8. **Technology** Use of outdated technology is often stated as a serious problem of such enterprises. This results in low productivity and uneconomical production.

9. **Sickness** Prevalence of sickness in small industries has become a point of worry for both the policy-makers and the entrepreneurs. The causes of sickness are both internal and external.

   - Internal problems include lack of skilled and trained labour, managerial and marketing skills.
   - External problems include delayed payment, shortage of working capital, inadequate loans and lack of demand for their products.

10. **Global Competition** In the present context of Liberalisation, Privatisation and Globalisation (LPG) policies being followed by several countries across the world. Small businesses feel threatened from the global entrepreneurs in the following are as

    - Competitions from medium and large industries as well as multinational companies.
    - High quality standards, technological skills, financial credit worthiness, managerial and marketing capabilities of large industries.
    - Due to strict requirements of quality certification like ISO 9,000, small industries have limited access to markets of developed countries.

Government Assistance to Small Business Units

Government, both at the central and state level, has been actively participating in promoting self employment opportunities. With respect to this, it has introduced various schemes and has extended institutional support to the small and rural industries.

Forms of support offered to small industries by the Government are stated below

- Institutional support in respect of credit facilities.
- Provision of developed sites for construction of sheds.
- Provision of training facilities.
- Supply of machinery on hire export marketing.
- Technical and financial assistance for technological upgradation.
- Special incentives for setting up of enterprises in backward areas.

Institutional Support to SSIs

The government has extended institutional support to SSIs by opening special institutions which cater to the financial and other needs of the SSIs.

The various institutions which help in the growth and development of SSIs are discussed below

National Small Industries Corporation (NSIC)

This was set up in 1955 to promote, aid and foster the growth of small-scale units in India.

If performs the following functions

- It supplies indigenous and imported machines and raw materials to small scale industries on hire-purchase schemes.
- It exports the product of small units and help to establish their credit worthiness.
- It helps in upgradation of technology.
- It provides mentoring and advisory services.
- It serves as technology business incubator.
- It develops software technology parks and technology transfer centres.
- It launches various schemes and extends support to help small scale entrepreneurs.

Various Schemes and Support Programmes launched by NSIC

1. **Performance and Credit Rating Scheme** It involves sensitising the small industries about the need of credit rating and encouraging the small business units to maintain good financial track record.

2. **Marketing Support Extended to MSMEs** NSIC extends marketing support to MSMEs through the following activities

- NSIC organises international technology exhibitions in foreign countries where micro, small and medium enterprises can showcase their products.
- NSIC also organises domestic exhibitions where MSMEs can showcase their products.
- Support for co-sponsoring of exhibitions organised by other organisations/industry/associations/ agencies.
- NSIC organises buyer-seller meets for MSMEs, where bulk and departmental buyers such as the railways, defence, large companies, etc are invited.
- NSIC conducts intensive campaigns to spread awareness regarding the various schemes of the government which are for the benefit of micro, small and medium enterprises.

3. **Other support to MSMEs**
   - Printing brochures and catalogues and preparing CDs and short films to spread information related to the products offered by MSMEs.
   - Development of websites which help MSMEs to market their products.
   - Development and disbursement of material which spreads awareness related to various programmes.
   - Preparing a directory which contains updated information related to various MSMEs.
   - Conducting studies to explore and access new markets, businesses and product ranges for both domestic and international markets.
   - Hosting international delegations and networking events.

District Industries Centre (DIC)

The district industries centre programme was launched on 1st May, 1978, with a view to provide all the services and support facilities to entrepreneurs, to set up small and village industries at district level.

Support Functions by DIC

- Identification of suitable schemes for the entrepreneurs interested to set up small industries in rural areas.
- Preparing feasibility reports for proposed projects.
- Helping the entrepreneurs in arranging for credit.
- Helping the entrepreneurs to have access to raw material and machinery.
- Extending various support services to entrepreneurs.

Some other Institutional Support to SSIs

1. **National Bank for Agriculture and Rural Development** (NABARD) The NABARD was set up on 15th July, 1982 to provide finance to rural areas in order to promote integrated rural development. It is an apex institution that provides finance to rural and small industries and organises training and development programmes for rural entrepreneurs.

2. **The Rural Small Business Development Centre** (RSBDC) It was set up by the world association for small and medium enterprises and is sponsored by NABARD. It aims at providing managerial and technical support to current and prospective micro and small entrepreneurs in rural areas.

   It has organised various programmes on rural entrepreneurship, skill upgradation workshops, training programmes and counselling camps in various villages.

3. **Rural and Women Entrepreneurship Development** (RWED) **Programme** This programme encourages rural people and women to establish entrepreneurial ventures. It aims at promoting a conducive business environment and in building human capacities to support entrepreneurial initiatives.

   It provides the following services
   - Creating a business environment which encourages initiative of rural and women entrepreneurs.
   - To enhance human and institutional capacities.
   - To provide training for women entrepreneurs.
   - To render other advisory services.

4. **Scheme of Fund for Regeneration of Traditional Industries** (SFURTI) A special fund has been created by the government to make the traditional industries more productive and competitive. The government started this fund in 2005 by investing ₹ 100 crore.

   This scheme is implemented by the ministry of agro and rural industries, in collaboration with state governments. The main objectives of this scheme are
   - To improve the technology of traditional units.
   - To create sustained employment opportunities.
   - To set up traditional industries in various parts of the country.

Chapter Practice

Objective Questions

• Multiple Choice Questions

1. People who own, operate and take risk of a business venture is called ....
  (a) aptitude (b) employee
  (c) entrepreneur (d) entrepreneurship
Ans. (c) entrepreneur

2. The main objective of entrepreneurship development is to
  (a) to increase literacy
  (b) to increase number of entrepreneurs
  (c) to increase GDP
  (d) All of the above
Ans. (b) to increase number of entrepreneurs

3. Entrepreneurship development leads to the establishment of industries. This helps in .... .
  (a) capital formation (b) economic growth
  (c) Both (a) and (b) (d) None of these
Ans. (c) Both (a) and (b)

4. .... is the single point of contact for the entire start-up ecosystem to enable knowledge exchange and funding access.
  (a) Start India fund (b) Start India forum
  (c) Start India hub (d) Start India meeting
Ans. (c) Start India hub

5. Sundeep is individual with surplus cash and interested to invest in upcoming start-ups. Which method is suitable for him?
  (a) Crowd funding (b) Venture capital
  (c) Boot strapping (d) Angel investment
Ans. (d) Angel investment

6. .... is the funding a project by raising money from a large number of people for a common goal.
  (a) Boot strapping (b) Crowdsourcing
  (c) Venture capitals (d) Angel investments
Ans. (b) Crowdsourcing

7. A business centre that offers working space and specialised support for new start ups is known as
  (a) Isolator (b) Injector (c) Incubator (d) Integrator
Ans. (c) Incubators provide professional services that facilitates the development of new business by providing resources like working space etc., support and advice.

8. **Statement I** The purpose of geographical indications is to encourage innovation in manufacturing field.
  Statement II Certification mark certifies the quality of product.
  Alternatives
  (a) Statement I is correct and Statement II is wrong
  (b) Statement II is correct and Statement I is wrong
  (c) Both the statements are correct
  (d) Both the statements are incorrect
Ans. (b) The purpose of geographical indications is to encourage innovation in the scientific field.

9. A ...... is an exclusive right granted by government which provides the exclusive right to exclude all others and prevent them from using or offering from sale.
  (a) copyrights (b) patent
  (c) proprietary rights (d) trademark
Ans. (b) patent

10. Literary work is protected under
  (a) Patent (b) Trademark
  (c) Copyright (d) Crowd funding
Ans. (c) Copyright

11. **Statement I** Entrepreneurship development leads to concentration of economic activities in few areas of the country.
  Statement II For start-ups, there will be government inspection regarding such compliance from second year onwards.
  Alternatives
  (a) Statement I is correct and Statement II is wrong
  (b) Statement II is correct and Statement I is wrong
  (c) Both the statements are correct
  (d) Both the statements are incorrect
Ans. (d) Entrepreneurship development leads to scattering of economic activities in all areas of the country. There is no government inspection of such start-ups regarding such compliance for first three years.

12. .... provides subsidised loans to youth to establish their business if their family income is less than ₹ 1,00,000.
(a) Prime Minister Vikas Yojana
(b) Prime Minister Business Scheme
(c) Prime Minister Grameen Yojana
(d) Prime Minister Rozgar Yojana

Ans. (d) Prime Minister Rozgar Yojana

13. In India, industries are classified on the basis of investment in plant and machinery. Amount of .... in a village industry per head artisan cannot exceed is ₹ 50,000.
(a) working capital investment
(b) cash investment
(c) fixed capital investment
(d) Both (a) and (c)

Ans. (c) fixed capital investment

14. Statement I Small business has generally short gestation period.

Statement II Small scale industries are considered good for countries that have less labour and surplus capital.
Alternatives
(a) Statement I is correct and Statement II is wrong
(b) Statement II is correct and Statement I is wrong
(c) Both the statements are correct
(d) Both the statements are incorrect

Ans. (a) Small scale industries are considered good for countries like India, that have surplus labour and less capital.

15. M/s ABS is a small enterprise engaged in the production of springs. It supplies its entire output to tractor manufactures. M/s ABS can be classified as a
(a) ancillary industry
(b) tiny industry
(c) secondary industry
(d) traditional industry

Ans. (a) Any enterprise which supplies not less than 50% of its total production to any other industry is known as 'ancilliary industry'.

16. M/s XYZ a small scale enterprise has following investments in its business

Research and development cost	₹ 3 lakh
Plant and machinery	₹ 8 lakh
Factory shed	₹ 5 lakh
Industrial safety equipments	₹ 3 lakh
Land	₹ 10 lakh

Decide the category to which M/s XYZ belongs?
(a) micro enterprise
(b) small enterprise
(c) medium enterprise
(d) cottage industry

Ans. (a) M/s XYZ belongs to micro enterprise because its total investment is only ₹ 23 lakh (i.e. cost of Plant and machinery + Factory shed + Land). Research and development cost and industrial saftey equipments are not the part of investment in plant and machinery.

17. Statement I Small industries are able to maintain good personal relations with customers.

Statement II Small scale industries suffer from lack of adequate working capital.
Alternatives
(a) Statement I is correct and Statement II is wrong
(b) Statement II is correct and Statement I is wrong
(c) Both the statements are correct
(d) Both the statements are incorrect

Ans. (c) Small scale industries have the inherent strength of adaptability and have personal touch with both customers and employees. Due to delayed payment from customers and locking up of their capital in unsold stocks, small units suffer from lack of adequate working capital. Banks also do not provide funds to them.

18. .... institution is setup as an Apex Bank to provide direct/indirect financial assistance under different schemes and also coordinates the functions of other institution in similar activities.
(a) SIDBI
(b) IDBI
(c) NSIC
(d) NABARD

Ans. (a) SIDBI

19. Government at various levels are providing assistance to small businesses by various means. By helping small industries, government aims at
(a) prevention of migration
(b) poverty alleviation
(c) employment to artisans
(d) All of these

Ans. (d) By providing assistance to small business, government aims to achieve various targets by a single means. When industries are established in rural areas, people don't have to move to cities in order to find work and on the other hand, rural poor and artisans get job. Therefore, it can be said that by helping small business, government achieves all of these goals.

20. Which institution is at top of hierarchy in the administrative setup for the promotion and development of the small scale, agro and rural industries?
(a) SIDO
(b) NSIC
(c) Ministry of MSME
(d) Ministry of Industrial Affairs

Ans. (c) Ministry of MSME

• Assertion–Reasoning MCQs

Directions (Q. Nos. 1 to 7) *There are two statements marked as Assertion (A) and Reason (R). Read the statements and choose the appropriate option from the options given below*

(a) Both Assertion (A) and Reason (R) are true and Reason (R) is the correct explanation of Assertion (A)

(b) Both Assertion (A) and Reason (R) are true, but Reason (R) is not the correct explanation of Assertion (A)

(c) Assertion (A) is true, but Reason (R) is false

(d) Assertion (A) is false, but Reason (R) is true

1. Assertion (A) Entrepreneurship development is considered as a continuous process.

Reason (R) Entrepreneurship development involves learning which is a never-ending process.

Ans. (a) Both Assertion (A) and Reason (R) are true and Reason (R) is the correct explanation of Assertion (A)

2. Assertion (A) Entrepreneurship development helps in capital formation of country.

Reason (R) Entrepreneurs develop and produce substituted products of imported goods and prevent the over-dependence on the other countries.

Ans. (b) It encourage the establishment of new industries in economy which increase in the capital formation rate in country.

3. Assertion (A) The industrial units for whom the output is manufactured are referred to as 'main units'.

Reason (R) Ancillary small industrial unit manufactures parts, components, sub-assemblies, tools or intermediate products for other industrial units.

Ans. (d) The industrial units for whom the output is manufactured are referred to as 'parent units'.

4. Assertion (A) Small scale industries can be opened anywhere in the country, without any locational constraints and the benefits of industrialisation can be reoped by every region.

Reason (R) The latent skills and talents of people can be channelled into business ideas, which can be converted into reality with little or nil capital investment anywhere.

Ans. (c) These industries produce products using simple technologies and depend on locally available resources in terms of both material and labour, thus, they can be opened anywhere in the country, without any locational constraints.

5. Assertion (A) Small scale industries enjoy the advantage of low cost of production.

Reason (R) The establishment and running cost of small-scale industries are minimum. Locally available resources are less expensive.

Ans. (a) Both Assertion (A) and Reason (R) are true and Reason (R) is the correct explanation of Assertion (A)

6. Assertion (A) Entrepreneurship development helps in generating employment opportunities.

Reason (R) Entrepreneurship development enables the economy to utilise and explore the abundant of natural resources.

Ans. (b) Entrepreneurship development enables entrepreneurs to create more/additional employment opportunities for youth by creating more businesses and workplaces.

7. Assertion (A) Small scale industries capture the opportunity at the right time by saving time correctly.

Reason (R) Small scale industries are small in size, which allows them to take quick decisions.

Ans. (a) Both Assertion (A) and Reason (R) are true and Reason (R) is the correct explanation of Assertion (A)

• Case Based MCQs

1. Direction *Read the following text and answer the question no. (i) to (vi) on the basis of the same.*

Mayank, after completing his master's degree in management, decided to start his own enterprise with the name Mayank Food Industries in his village in Himachal Pradesh and opted for labour-intensive techniques to provide employment to local people.

He took the help of DIC, a government institution for promoting small scale industries to get knowledge about incentives and schemes launched by the government for opening small scale industries. It was estimated that, the food and beverages plant to be set up will require a fixed capital investment of ₹ 80 lakhs.

The working capital requirements is estimated to be ₹ 20 lakhs. The directors of the company decided to raise the capital by issuing shares as well as taking loans from financial institutions. In addition to this, to thrive the business, the directors decided to take benefit of various policies and programmes formulated by the ministry.

With all these products, they were able to produce extremely high quality and delicious food recipes. This led to creation of intellectual property right for the firm.

(i) The category into which this industry will be placed under MSMED Act is

(a) micro enterprises

(b) small scale manufacturing enterprises

(c) small service enterprises

(d) medium enterprises

Ans. (b) small scale manufacturing enterprises

(ii) The Directors of the company decided to raise the capital by issuing shares as well as taking loans from financial institutions. The shares are the example of ……… capital source.
(a) internal, long-term   (b) external, long-term
(c) internal, borrowed   (d) external, borrowed

Ans. (a) internal, long-term

(iii) Mayank has entrepreneurship skills as shown in above case. Which of the following indicates entrepreneurship?
(a) Setting up one's own business
(b) Pursuing employment
(c) Practising profession
(d) All of the above

Ans. (a) Setting up one's own business

(iv) DIC stands for which of the following?
(a) District Industrial Centre
(b) Development and Industrial Corporation
(c) Department of Infrastructure and Capital Formation
(d) None of the above

Ans. (a) District Industrial Centre

(v) Which organisation is responsible for implementing and monitoring various policies and programmes formulated by the ministry of micro, small and medium enterprises?
(a) NSIC   (b) SIDBI
(c) NABARD   (d) SIDO

Ans. (d) SIDO

(vi) "With all these products, they were able to produce extremely high quality and delicious food recipes." Which IPR is highlighted in this line?
(a) Patents   (b) Copyrights
(c) Trademarks   (d) Trade secrets

Ans. (d) Trade secrets

2. Direction *Read the following text and answer the question no. (i) to (vi) on the basis of the same.*

Three friends, after completing their graduation, decided to open their own business and to create employment opportunities for others too. After their meeting with the manager of DIC, they attended entrepreneurship development programme. As a result of their entrepreneurship, Zayka Food Industries is created and operated successfully by them.

To create a feeling of belongingness in the customers and for branding purposes, they started to use 'hat' as a symbol on all their products. Soon, this become an intellectual property for the company. After getting a good response in the market, now one of them is planning to set up a new unit "Laajwaab Foods and Beverages Industry" in rural area of Odisha and opted for labour intensive technique, due to easy availability of cheap labour.

The finance manager has estimated the investment of ₹ 2 crore to acquire plant and machinery and ₹ 80 lakhs for meeting operating expenses of this new unit. The company did not want to dilute the ownership and did not want any interference from investors/lenders. Also, it expects good cash flow return from the new unit.

For arrangement of finance and availing professional services that facilitates the development of new business, they approached a body which is located in their universities.

(i) Which category of SSI, "Lajawaab Foods and Beverage Industries" belongs to?
(a) Micro enterprises   (b) Small enterprises
(c) Medium enterprises   (d) Cottage industry

Ans. (b) Small enterprises

(ii) Which of the following is not a feature of entrepreneurship?
(a) Systematic activity   (b) Risk element
(c) Profession   (d) Dynamic process

Ans. (c) Profession

(iii) Post-training stage of ED programme does not include
(a) Management Skill Development
(b) Guidance in Project Implementation
(c) Sustaining Motivation
(d) Providing-follow up

Ans. (a) Management Skill Development

(iv) The finance manager has estimated the investment of ₹ 2 crore to acquire plant and machinery and ₹ 80 lakh for meeting operating expenses of this new unit. The company did not want to dilute the ownership and did not want any interference from investors/lenders. Also, it expects good cash flow return from the new unit. Which form of capital would be better for the company?
(a) Equity capital   (b) Long-term loans
(c) Preference capital   (d) Loans from commercial bank

Ans. (b) Long-term loans

(v) "For arrangement of finance and availing professional services that facilitates the development of new business, they approached a body which is located in their universities." Which way to fund start-up is highlighted here?
(a) Accelerators   (b) Incubators
(c) Private equity   (d) Venture capital

Ans. (b) Incubators

(vi) "To create a feeling of belongingness in the customers and for branding purposes, they started to use 'hat' as a symbol on all their products." Which IPR is highlighted in the line?

(a) Patents   (b) Copyrights
(c) Trademarks   (d) Trade secrets

Ans. (c) Trademarks

3. Direction *Read the following text and answer the question no. (i) and to (vi) on the basis of the same.*

Siraj is a handicraft artist. He has been doing the work for different firms for more than 10 years. Now, he has decided to set up his own enterprise in his small town.

He has employed three local people and invested ₹ 5 lakh. He has received lot of assistance with government policies. The raw materials are sourced from the nearby villages. The firm is known to produce products as per the individual customer tastes and preferences. The goods are sold at a cheap price because cost of production is low. However, as the business is growing, Siraj is finding it difficult to manage all the work since he has never managed business to such an extent.

In the recent times, company has also faced the problem of arranging finance for funding increasing purchase orders of big tickets. But to his rescue, he got finance from an institution that provides finance to rural and small industries and organises training and development programmes for rural entrepreneurs.

However, he has now got a new problem at hand. One of the big textiles players has entered this handicraft space and has started poaching Siraj's employees at higher salaries. Siraj is now seeking a solution to this.

(i) In which category, Siraj's firm falls into?
(a) Micro enterprises   (b) Small enterprises
(c) Medium enterprises   (d) None of these

Ans. (a) Investment is less than ₹ 25,00,000.

(ii) "He has received lot of assistance with government policies." Which ministry is the nodal ministry for formulation of policy and coordination of central assistance for the promotion and development of small scale industries in India?
(a) Ministry of micro enterprises
(b) Ministry of small enterprises
(c) Ministry of medium enterprises
(d) None of the above

Ans. (d) Ministry of Micro, Small and Medium Enterprises

(iii) Which role of small scale industries in India is highlighted in the passage?

(a) Balanced regional growth
(b) Low cost of production
(c) Customised production
(d) All of the above

Ans. (d) **Balanced Regional Growth** The raw materials are sourced from the nearby villages.

Customised Production The firm is known to produce products as per the individual customer tastes and preferences.

Low Cost of Production The goods are sold at a cheap price because cost of production is low.

(iv) Which problem of small scale industries is highlighted in the line, "Siraj is finding it difficult to manage all the work since he has never managed business to such an extent"?
(a) Quality   (b) Capacity utilisation
(c) Managerial skills   (d) Finance

Ans. (c) Managerial skills

(v) "He got finance from an institution that provides finance to rural and small industries and organises training and development programmes for rural entrepreneurs." Which institution is highlighted in this line?
(a) NSIC   (b) RSBDC
(c) NABARD   (d) Ministry of MSMEs

Ans. (c) NABARD

(vi) One of the big textiles players has entered this handicraft space and has started poaching Siraj's employees at higher salaries. Which problem of small business is highlighted in this line?
(a) Managerial skills   (b) Labour
(c) Finance   (d) Quality

Ans. (b) Labour

PART 2

Subjective Questions

• Short Answer (SA) Type Questions

1. What is meant by entrepreneurship development? Explain.

Ans. Entrepreneurship development refers to the process of enhancing entrepreneurial skills and knowledge through structured training and institution building programmes. It focuses on individual who wishes to start or expand a business.

The whole point of entrepreneurship development is to increase number of entrepreneurs and to create entrepreneurship culture within society. One trained entrepreneur can guide other on how to start their own enterprises. Now-a-days, it is treated as an important tool of industrialisation and a solution of unemployment in country.

2. Chris and Craig were having a discussion about entrepreneurship development. Chris suggested that there were no pre-requisites for entrepreneurship development whereas Craig suggested that there are some pre-requisites. Who – Chris or Craig is correct? Explain.

Ans. Craig is correct because there are some pre-requisites for entrepreneurship development. Following are the pre-requisites

(i) Intelligence (ii) Motivation
(iii) Knowledge (iv) Sustained efforts
(v) Human factor
(vi) Government assistance/Grant
(vii) Opportunity
(viii) Industrial technology

3. What is Entrepreneurship Development Process (EDP)?

Ans. EDP is a process to help an individual in strengthening his entrepreneurial motive and in acquiring skills and capabilities necessary for playing his entrepreneurial role effectively. EDP is not merely a training programme. It is a process to

(i) enhance the motivation, knowledge and skills of potential entrepreneurs.
(ii) reforming the entrepreneurial behaviour.
(iii) assist entrepreneurs to develop their own ventures.

4. The government has launched startup India scheme for promoting startup culture in the country. What are the major objectives of this scheme?

Ans. Following are the objectives of startup India scheme

(i) trigger an entrepreneurial culture, inculcate entrepreneurial values in the society at large and influence the mindset of people towards entrepreneurship.
(ii) create awareness about the charms of being an entrepreneur and the process of entrepreneurship, especially among the youth.
(iii) encourage more dynamic startups by motivating enducated youth, scientists and technologists to consider entrepreneurship as a lucrative, preferred and viable career.
(iv) support the early phase of entrepreneurship development, including the pre-startup, nascent, as well as, early post startup phase and growth enterprises.

5. What are some of the key action points of Start India Initiative?

Ans. Action points of Start India Initiatives are as follows (any three)

(i) **Simplification and Handholding** In order to make compliance for startups, friendly and flexible, simplifications are announced. Government of India has launched a mobile app and a website for easy online registration.

(ii) **Startup India Hub** The objective is to create a single point of contact for the entire startup ecosystem and enable knowledge exchange and access to funding. Start-up India Hub will be key stakeholder of entrepreneurs. It will be their friend, mentor and guide to hold their hand.

(iii) **Legal Support and Fast-tracking Patent Examination** The scheme for Startups Intellectual Property Protections (SIPP) is envisaged to facilitate protection of patents, trademarks and designs of innovative and interested startups.

(iv) **Easy Exit** In the event of a business failure and wind up of operations, procedures are being adopted to reallocate capital and resources towards more productive avenues. This will promote experimentation with new and innovative ideas, without fearing complex and long drawn exit process. A start-up can close its business within 90 days from the date of application of winding up.

6. Sana and Vishal are friends who have been planning for a start-up. With the money they had, they did initial research and proof of concept. To fund their idea, a professionally managed fund institution provided them the funding. Identify this source to fund the start-up and explain.

Ans. The way to fund the start-up highlighted is venture capital. Venture capital are professionally managed funds who invest in companies that have huge potential in future.

They focus on sale rather than profit of ventures. This type of funding is often obtained in exchange for an equity stake in business. Generally, such funding is involved in software, technology and bio-technology. It bridges the gap where traditional sources of funds cannot participate actively in funding new venture. e.g., Nexus Venture Partner, Kalaari Capital, Accel Partners.

7. ST foods Inc is a company preparing Rajasthani food. The company has 23 outlets in Rajasthan and Gujarat. The company prepares its foods with recipes unique to it and uniform across outlets. These recipes have been the driving force of business and are not known to general public. Identify and explain the intellectual property right discussed.

Ans. The IPR discussed is trade secret.

It is an information that

(i) is not generally known to public.
(ii) confers economic benefit.
(iii) is the subject of reasonable efforts by the holder to maintain its secrecy.

For example CoCa Cola's recipe is trade secret. KFC keep secret ingredients in its recipe.

(iv) is protected without any procedural formalities for an unlimited period.

8. Write short note on

   (i) Design

   (ii) Plant variety

   (iii) Semiconductor Integrated Circuits Layout Design

Ans. (i) **Design** A 'design' includes shape, pattern, and arrangement of lines or colour combination that is applied to any article. It is a protection given to aesthetic appearance or eye-catching features. The term of protection of a design is valid for 10 years, which can be renewed for further 5 years after expiration of this term, during which a registered design can only be used after getting a license from its owner and once the validity period is over, the design is in public domain.

   (ii) **Plant Variety** It is essentially grouping plants into categories based on their botanical characteristics. It is a type of variety which is bred and developed by farmers. This helps in conserving, improving and making available plant genetic resources. For example, hybrid versions of potatoes.

   (iii) **Semiconductor Integrated Circuits Layout Design** A semiconductor layout design means a layout of transistors and other circuitry elements used and formed on a semiconductor material, as an insulating material, or inside the semiconductor material. Its design is to perform an electronic circuitry function.

9. Identify any six major industries that are grouped in the small-scale sector of India.

Ans. Six major industries are

   (i) Food product

   (ii) Chemical and chemical products

   (iii) Leather and leather products

   (iv) Hosiery and garments

   (v) Repair services

   (vi) Beverages, tobacco and tobacco products

10. What are the three types of enterprises with respect to manufacturing?

Ans. The three types of enterprises with respect to manufacturing are

   (i) **Micro Enterprise** In micro enterprise, the investment in plant and machinery does not exceed ₹ 25 lakh.

   (ii) **Small Enterprise** In small enterprise, the investment in plant and machinery is more than ₹ 25 lakh but does not exceed ₹ 5 crore.

   (iii) **Medium Enterprise** In medium enterprise, the investment in plant and machinery is more than ₹ 5 crore but does not exceed ₹ 10 crore.

11. Service enterprises can be divided into three categories majorly. Mention about these categories.

Ans. Service enterprises are categorised as follows

   (i) **Micro Enterprise** In micro enterprise, the investment in equipment does not exceed ₹ 10 lakh.

   (ii) **Small Enterprise** In small enterprise, the investment in equipment is more than ₹ 10 lakh but does not exceed ₹ 2 crore.

   (iii) **Medium Enterprise** In medium enterprise, the investment in equipment is more than ₹ 2 crore but does not exceed ₹ 5 crore.

12. Differentiate between ancillary unit and tiny unit on any three basis.   **(NCERT)**

Ans. The differences between an ancillary unit and a tiny unit are

Basis	Ancillary Unit	Tiny Unit
Meaning	An ancillary unit is the unit which supplies not less than 50% of its production to the parent unit.	A tiny unit is the business enterprise whose investment in plant and machinery is not more than ₹ 25 lakh.
Investment Limit	Investment limit in such unit is ₹ 5 crore.	Investment limit is ₹ 25 lakh in this type of unit.
Assistance of Parent Unit	Parent unit assists the ancillary unit by providing technical and financial help.	No such assistance is there.

13. Highlight the importance of small scale industries in Indian employment and GDP context.

Ans. Following points highlight the importance of SSIs in Indian employment and GDP

   (i) **Contribution in GDP** Small industries in India account for 95% of the industrial units of the country. They contribute almost 40% of the gross industrial value added and 45% of the total exports (direct and indirect) from India.

   (ii) **Employment Generation** In India, small industries are the second largest employers of human resources, after agriculture. They generate more employment opportunities per unit of capital invested as compared to large industries. Thus, they are considered good for countries like India, that have surplus labour and less capital.

14. Apart from increasing the employment opportunities and adding to the GDP, small scale industries contribute and assist a country like India in numerous ways. Do you agree? Give reasons.

Ans. Yes, I agree with the statement that apart from increasing the employment opportunities and adding to the GDP, small scale industries contribute and assist a country like India in numerous ways. The reasons for the same are (any three)

   (i) **Supply Variety of Products** Small industries in our country supply enormous variety of products which include goods of mass consumption such as readymade garments, hosiery goods, stationery items, soaps and detergents, domestic utensils, etc. Sophisticated goods such as electrical goods, engineering goods, drugs, etc are also manufactured by these industries.

(ii) **Balanced Regional Development** As these industries produce products using simple technologies and depend on locally available resources in terms of both material and labour, thus, they can be opened anywhere in the country, without any locational constraints and the benefits of industrialisation can be reaped by every region.

(iii) **Provide Business Opportunities** They provide ample opportunity for entrepreneurship. The latent skills and talents of people can be channelled into business ideas, which can be converted into reality with little or nil capital investment.

(iv) **Low Cost of Production** They also enjoy the advantage of low cost of production. This is because the establishment and running cost are minimum. Locally available resources are less expensive. Due to lower cost of production, they have competitive strength.

15. Vijay runs his small factory for producing cotton goods. He wants to venture into other countries but could not. Moreover, some MNCs have come up in the country giving tough times to Vijay. Which problem of small scale industries is highlighted here?

Ans. In the given text, 'global competition' is highlighted as the problem of small scale industry.

Small businesses feel threatened from the global entrepreneurs in the following areas

(i) Competitions from medium and large industries as well as multinational companies.

(ii) High quality standards, technological skills, financial credit worthiness, managerial and marketing capabilities of large industries.

(iii) Due to strict requirements of quality certification like ISO 9,000, small industries have limited access to markets of developed countries.

16. Amar, Akbar and Anthony are three good friends who have completed a vocational course in entrepreneurship. After their school education finding the job market tough. They were contemplating the idea of setting up a small business using the skills they had learnt in their course. However, they knew very little about business.

They were wondering what business to start, where to locate it, how to procure machinery and materials needed for the business, how to raise money and how to market. They came across a notification given by the district industries centre located near the industrial estate in Balanagar Ranga Reddy District of Andhra Pradesh

regarding a seminar on government's assistance for a small business aimed at young entrepreneurs.

Excited with the news, the three friends decided to attend the seminar. They were told about the financial and other assistance offered by the central and state governments under the rural employment generation programme to the educated youth. They found that toys were in demand and decided to manufacture toys. They started a small scale industry in their village by taking financial assistance with the help of khadi and village industries commission. Today, they are successful makers of toys and in the near future. They plan to get into export market as well.

(i) Which problems were faced by Amar, Akbar and Anthony, when they decided to set up a small business?

(ii) Which institutions helped Amar, Akbar and Anthony in establishing their small scale industry?

Ans. (i) Amar, Akbar and Anthony faced the following problems when they decided to set up a small business

(a) Problems related to identification of a business idea.

(b) Problems related to location of business.

(c) Problems related to procurement of materials and machines required for the business.

(d) Problems related to finance and marketing

(ii) Following institutions helped Amar, Akbar and Anthony in establishing their small scale industry

(a) District Industries Centre

(b) Khadi and Village Industries Commission

17. Explain in detail, the following three problems of small scale industries in the country

(i) Finance   (ii) Marketing

(iii) Raw Materials

Ans. (i) **Finance** One of the severe problems faced by SSIs is the non-availability of adequate finance to carry out its operations. These units lack in credit worthiness and have a small capital base. As a result, they heavily depend on local financial resources and frequently become the victims of exploitation by the money lenders.

(ii) **Marketing** Small scale enterprises are unable to meet the expenses of marketing activities. They depend on middlemen who exploit them by paying low prices for their goods and delaying their payments.

(iii) **Raw Materials** If the required materials are not available, small businesses have to compromise on the quality or have to pay high price to get good quality materials. Their bargaining power is relatively low due to the small quantity of purchases made by them. They cannot afford to buy in bulk because they do not have the facility to store material and neither do they have the necessary finance.

18. What are the different forms of support offered to small industries by the government?

Ans. Forms of support offered to small industries by the government are

(i) Institutional support in respect of credit facilities.

(ii) Provision of developed sites for construction of sheds.

(iii) Provision of training facilities.

(iv) Supply of machinery on hire export marketing.

(v) Technical and financial assistance for technological upgradation.

(vi) Special incentives for setting up of enterprises in backward areas.

19. 'Kamna' is SSI engaged in the manufacturing of handloom sarees. 60% of the share capital of this unit is jointly owned by Sumitra and her daughter Kamayani. What form of concessions is the above unit entitled to?

Ans. 'Kamna' is a women enterprise. If a small scale industry's more than 51% share capital is owned by women or a group of women, individually or jointly, then it is referred to as a 'women enterprise'. Such types of enterprises can avail the following concessions from the government

(i) Low rate of interest on loans

(ii) Easy repayment facility.

20. Write a short note on

(i) Small Industries Development Organisation

(ii) National Small Industries Corporation

Ans. (i) **Small Industries Development Organisation** (SIDO) This organisation is also referred to as office of the development commissioner, SSI. It is attached to the ministry of micro, small and medium enterprises and is responsible for implementing and monitoring various policies and programmes formulated by the ministry.

(ii) **National Small Industries Corporation** (NSIC) It is a public sector enterprise of the ministry of micro, small and medium enterprises and has been providing marketing support to the medium and small industries under the marketing assistance scheme.

21. Explain the two banks established by the support of government for the purpose of development of small-scale industries and rural development.

Ans. The two banks are NABARD and SIDBI

(i) **National Bank for Agriculture and Rural Development** (NABARD) The NABARD was set up on 15th July, 1982 to provide finance to rural areas in order to promote integrated rural development. It is an apex institution that provides finance to rural and small industries and organises training and development programmes for rural entrepreneurs.

(ii) **Small Industries Development Bank of India** (SIDBI) It was established in April, 1990 as a wholly owned subsidiary of IDBI, under the Small Industries Development Bank of India Act, 1990. Its main object is to promote, finance and develop the small scale sector in India. It provides direct and indirect financial assistance to small business organisations under various schemes. It coordinates the functions of other institutions engaged in similar activities.

22. Under NCEUS, what issues are being considered?

Ans. Following issues are being considered under National Commission for Enterprises in Unorganised Secotor

(i) Growth poles for the informal sector in the form of clusters, in order to get external economic aid.

(ii) Potential for public private partnership in imparting the skills required by the informal sector.

(iii) Provision of micro finance and related services to the informal sector.

(iv) Providing social security to the workers in the informal sector.

• Long Answer (LA) Type Questions

1. Explain the characteristics of entrepreneurship in detail.

Ans. The following are the characteristics of entrepreneurship

(i) **Systematic Activity** Entrepreneurship has certain temperamental, skill and other knowledge and competency requirements that can be acquired, learnt and developed, both by formal educational and vocational training as well as by observation and work experience.

(ii) **Lawful and Purposeful Activity** The object of entrepreneurship is lawful business. It is important to take note that one may try to legitimise unlawful actions as entrepreneurship on the grounds that just as entrepreneurship entails risk, so does illicit businesses.

(iii) **Innovation** Entrepreneurship is creative in the sense that it involves innovation, introduction of new products, discovery of new markets and sources of supply of inputs, technological breakthroughs as well as introduction of newer organisational forms for doing things better, cheaper, faster and in the present context, in a manner that causes the least harm to the ecology/ environment.

(iv) **Organisation of Production** Entrepreneur, in response to a perceived business opportunity, mobilises the resources into a productive enterprise or firm. In an economy with a well-developed financial system, he has to convince just the funding institutions and with the capital so arranged he may enter into contracts of supply of equipment, materials, utilities (such as water and electricity) and technology.

(v) **Risk-taking** Entrepreneurship involves risk as individuals opting for a career in entrepreneurship take a bigger risk that is involved in a career in employment or practice of a profession as there is no 'assured' payoff. However, entrepreneurs are so sure of their capabilities that they can convert situations with higher risks into opportunities.

2. According to ILO's latest report, the number of the unemployed in country will increase to 18.6 million in 2018 and 18.9 million in 2019 against 18.3 million in 2017. The International Labour Organisation (ILO) has said in its latest report that India could witness a higher unemployment rate of 3.5% in 2018, a little more than that of 3.4% as projected earlier. Exports are saying that unemployment is up because "Make in India", "Start-up India" and other official schemes are not working in proper manner due to lack of entrepreneurial skills among the youth.

(i) Identify the concept which can reduce the unemployment problem of India.

(ii) State the need of this concept in India.

Ans. (i) Entrepreneurship development can reduce the unemployment problem in India.

(ii) For a developing economy like India, need of entrepreneurship development arises due to the following reasons

(a) **Eliminates Poverty and Unemployment** The basic problem of India is poverty and unemployment, Entrepreneurship development can help the unemployed youth to opt for self-employment and entrepreneurial as a career.

(b) **Capital Formation** The various development banks like IDBI, IFCI, SIDBI take initiative in promoting entrepreneurship through fund. Entrepreneurship development encourage the establishment of new industries in economy which is a cause of capital formation.

(c) **Improvement in Per Capita Income** Entrepreneurship development encourages new startups which is big cause of increase in per capita income of India.

(d) **Defuses Social Tension** Entrepreneurship development can help channelising the talent and energies of frustrated unemployed youth of India. In other words, it can raise harmony within society.

(e) **Discovering New Markets** It helps the entrepreneurs in discovering new market in country and outside country.

(f) **Helpful in Selection of Project and Product** It helps entrepreneurs in evaluating various projects and products and choose the most suitable one which can be established and started easily, gives maximum profit with least possible risk and which have scope for further development.

3. Ritvik is a graduate from University of Delhi. He decided to start-up just after the graduation. He took on going edtech wave in his stride and set up a blended (offline + online) model of learning extra-curricular activities. He started boot strapped with the savings of his internship stipend. However, he is struggling to expand on the model because of lack of funds. Suggest him six ways to raise more capital.

Ans. Ways for him to raise capital are

(i) **Bank Loan** Funding from bank will involve the usual process of sharing the business plan and the valuation details, along with project report based on which the loan is sanctioned.

(ii) **Government Programmes that Offers Start-up Capital** Most popular scheme is Pradhan Mantri Micro Units Development and Refinance Agency Limited (MUDRA) which started with an initial corpus of ₹ 20,000 crore to extend benefits to around 10 Lakh SMEs.

(iii) **Angel Funding** Angel Investments take very early-stage business under their wing while venture capital or equity investors do not like to commit capital to tiny business. Many household names, like Google, Facebook were financed in their earliest stages by angel investors. e.g. Mumbai Angels, Hyderabad Angels Lets Venture, etc.

(iv) **Venture Capital** These are professionally managed funds who invest in companies that have huge potential in future. They focus on sale rather than profit of ventures. This type of funding is often obtained in exchange for an equity stake in business. e.g. Nexus Venture Partner, Kalaari Capital, Accel Partners.

(v) **Incubators** They provide professional services that facilitates the development of new business by providing resources, support and advice. In India, more than 50% of the incubators are located in universities indicating role of universities in supporting new start-ups. e.g.,

    (a) Innovation and Entrepreneurship (SINE), IIT Mumbai

    (b) Technology Business Incubator IIT Delhi

(vi) **Accelerators** These are organisations that offer a range of support service and funding opportunities for startups. They provide capital and investment in return for start-up equity. They target set action to boost the development and growth of a startups. e.g.

    (a) Amity Innovation Incubator

    (b) IAN Business Incubator, Kyron

4. What do you mean by intellectual property rights? Also, explain its importance.

Ans. Intellectual property rights are the intellectuals emerged from the human mind and the legal right on these human intellects. It is used to protect brand name, design, technology.

Importance of Intellectual Property Rights is as follows

(i) Exclusive right on the use of IP is the biggest motivation behind creation of intellectual property.

(ii) Customers get improved goods and services due to IPR.

(iii) Entrepreneurs are enabled to earn more revenue due to IPR.

(iv) It is cost saving mechanism for society through effectively utilisation of resources.

(v) In India, the union cabinet on 13th May, 2016 approved the national intellectual property right policy to promote entrepreneurs.

5. What do you mean by rural industry? Also, explain its features.

Ans. Rural industry is also known as cottage industry or traditional industry. It is not defined by capital investment criteria as in the case of other small scale industries. However, cottage industries are characterised by certain features which are as follows

Following are the features of cottage industry

(i) It is organised by individuals, with private resources.

(ii) It normally uses family labour and locally available talent and is labour intensive.

(iii) In cottage industry, simple equipments are in use.

(iv) In it, capital investment is small.

(v) It produces simple products, normally in their own premises.

(vi) It produces goods using indigenous technology.

6. Small scale industries play a pivotal role in rural economy of a country. Comment.

Ans. The role of small scale industries in rural India is explained in the following points

(i) **Non-farm Employment** Traditionally, rural households in India were exclusively engaged in agriculture. But now, rural households have varied and multiple sources of income, and participate in a wide range of non-agricultural activities alongwith the traditional rural activities of farming and agricultural labour. This can be largely attributed to the setting up of agro-based rural small industries.

(ii) **Employment for Artisans** Cottage and rural industries play an important role in providing employment opportunities in the rural areas, especially to the traditional artisans and the weaker sections of society.

(iii) **Prevention of Migration** Development of rural and village industries can also prevent migration of rural population to urban areas in search of employment.

(iv) **Poverty Alleviation** Village and small industries are significant as producers of consumer goods and absorbers of surplus labour, thereby addressing the problems of supply, poverty and unemployment.

(v) **Promoting SSI and Rural Industrialisation** Promotion of small scale industries and rural industrialisation has been considered by the Government of India as a powerful instrument for realising the twin objectives of "accelerated industrial growth and creating additional productive employment potential in rural and backward areas."

(vi) **Socio-economic Aspects** These industries contribute towards socio-economic aspects such as reduction in income inequalities, dispersed development of industries and linkage with other sectors of the economy.

7. Small-scale industries have got some inherent problems. These are the problems which have been in system for many years now and make the development of small scale industries much more challenging. Discuss any six such problems.

Ans. Problems of small-scale industries are

(i) **Managerial Skills** Small business is generally promoted and operated by a single person, who may not possess technical and managerial skills to run the business.

(ii) **Labour** Due to low remuneration, talented people are not attracted to work with small business, firms as they cannot afford to pay higher salaries to the employees.

This affects employee willingness to work hard and produce more. Thus, productivity per employee is relatively low and employee turnover is generally high.

(iii) **Quality** Many small business organisations do not adhere to desired standards of quality. Instead, they concentrate on cutting the cost and keeping the prices low. As they do not maintain quality, they are not able to compete in global markets.

(iv) **Capacity Utilisation** Due to lack of marketing skills leading to lack of demand, many small business firms have to operate below full capacity due to which their operating costs tend to increase. This leads to sickness and closure of the business.

(v) **Technology** Use of outdated technology is often stated as a serious problem of such enterprises. This results in low productivity and uneconomical production.

(vi) **Sickness** Prevalence of sickness in small industries has become a point of worry for both the policy-makers and the entrepreneurs. The causes of sickness are both internal and external.

   (a) Internal problems include lack of skilled and trained labour, managerial and marketing skills.

   (b) External problems include delayed payment, shortage of working capital, inadequate loans and lack of demand for their products.

8. Discuss any six incentives provided by Central/State Government for setting up small scale units in backward or hilly areas. **(NCERT)**

Ans. Some of the common incentives provided by the government for industries in backward and hilly areas are (any six)

(i) **Land** Every state offers developed plots for setting up of industries. The terms and conditions may vary. Some states don't charge rent in the initial years, while some allow payment in instalments.

(ii) **Power** Power is supplied at a concessional rate of 50 percent, while some states exempt such units from payment in the initial years.

(iii) **Water** Water is supplied on no-profit, no-loss basis or with 50 percent concession or exemption from water charges for a period of 5 years.

(iv) **Sales Tax** In all Union Territories, industries are exempted from sales tax, while some states extend exemption for 5 years period.

(v) **Octroi** Most states have abolished octroi.

(vi) **Raw Materials** Units located in backward areas get preferential treatment in the matter of allotment of scarce raw materials like cement, iron, steel, etc.

(vii) **Finance** Subsidy of 10-15 percent is given for building capital assets. Loans are also offered at concessional rates.

(viii) **Marketing Assistance** Government tries to solve their marketing problem by improving information and also provide guarantee for sale of goods.

(ix) **Tax Holiday** Exemption from paying taxes for 5 or 10 years is given to industries established in backward, hilly and tribal areas.

Chapter Test

Multiple Choice Questions

1. Trade secret is the information that
   (i) confers economic benefits (ii) is generally known to public
   (iii) is subject to reasonable efforts by the holder to maintain its secrecy
   Alternatives
   (a) Both (i) and (ii) (b) Both (ii) and (iii) (c) Both (i) and (iii) (d) (i), (ii) and (iii)

2. For which of the following, copyright protection is not available?
   (a) Literary work (b) Music work (c) Artistic work (d) Assembling

3. The investment limit of SSIs does not exceed ……… .
   (a) ₹ 50,00,000 (b) ₹ 1,00,00,000 (c) ₹ 2,50,00,000 (d) ₹ 5,00,00,000

4. India is one of the fastest growing economies of the world. In order to give a further boost to India's growth, large scale industrial units are required. MSME are still relevant in Indian context because there is
   (a) high capital investment and high population (b) lack of population and higher capital investment
   (c) lack of capital investment and lack of population (d) lack of capital investment and higher population

5. **Statement I** Copyright is used for preventing the copy of original idea.
   Statement II Trademark helps in protection of scientific inventions.
   Alternatives
   (a) Statement I is correct and Statement II is wrong (b) Statement II is correct and Statement I is wrong
   (c) Both the statements are correct (d) Both the statements are incorrect

Short Answer (SA) Type Questions

1. Khana Kahazana is a popular show aired on Zee Network. It has a page on Facebook that goes by the name "Zee Khana Khazana" (here in after referred to as ZKK). The page is said to be dedicated to food and recently we (the community of food bloggers) found that they are regularly stealing photographs from food bloggers and websites for their features. Identify and explain the intellectual asset rights which are violated by ZKK.

2. Distinguish between a small scale business unit and large scale business unit on the basis of nature, type of labour, scale of operation and capital.

3. Write a short note on the following ways to fund start-up
   (i) Incubators (ii) Accelerators

4. 'Nut and Bolt' is a small-scale unit supplying 80% of its production to Action Tractors. State and explain to which category of SSI does 'Nut and Bolt' belong to?

5. Entrepreneurship does not emerge spontaneously. Rather, it is the outcome of a dynamic process of interaction between a person and his/her environment. Ultimately, the choice of entrepreneurship as a career lies with an individual, yet he/she must see it as a desirable, as well as, a feasible option. In the light of the statement, explain any four features of entrepreneurship.

Long Answer (LA) Type Questions

1. The National Small Industries Corporation Ltd. is a Government of India enterprise under the Ministry of Micro, Small and Medium Enterprises (MSME). It operates through a country wide network of offices and technical centres in the country. NSIC has a B2B web portal. The portal provides small and medium sized enterprises in India, an access to customers around the globe exclusively, once they get themselves listed with NSIC portal for an annual fee.

   The portal facilitates transactions between buyers and sellers without any intervention. It has features which will enable virtual buyer-seller meets and assist in request of quotations for business orders. It also host a database of small and medium companies' details, products, catalogues and pictures.
   (i) Write a short note on NSIC.
   (ii) The above text tells about the assistance provided by NSIC to the small and medium enterprises for marketing their products. Give any two more modes of marketing assistance provided by NSIC.

2. What role does SIDBI play in promoting SSIs?

Answers

Multiple Choice Questions

1. (c) 2. (d) 3. (b) 4. (d) 5. (a)

CHAPTER 03

Internal Trade

In this Chapter...

- Trade
- Internal Trade
- Wholesaler
- Retailers
- Fixed Shop-Large Retailers

Trade

It refers to buying and selling of goods and services with the objective of earning profit. It bridges the gap between the producer and the consumer. The importance of trade in modern times has increased, as new products are being developed everyday and are being made available for consumption throughout the world.

Classification of Trade

Trade can broadly be classified into two categories

1. **Internal Trade** Trade which takes place within a country is called internal trade.
2. **External Trade** Trade which takes place between two or more countries is called external trade.

Internal Trade

Internal trade means movement of goods within the boundaries of the nation or country. In such trade, all payments are received and made in the national currency. Internal trade aims at equitable distribution of goods within a nation speedily and at a reasonable cost.

Classification of Internal Trade

1. **Wholesale Trade** It refers to purchasing goods and services in large quantity from manufacturers and reselling them to retailers, who then sells them to the ultimate consumers.

   Chain of Wholesale Trade includes

   Manufacturers → Wholesalers → Retailers → Consumers

2. **Retail Trade** It refers to purchasing relatively small quantity of goods from wholesalers and selling them to ultimate consumers.

   Chain of Retail Trade includes

   Wholesalers → Retailers → Consumers

Wholesaler

Wholesale trade is performed by wholesalers. They serve as an important link between manufacturers and retailers.

Wholesaler provide various services to the manufacturers as well as the retailers, that are mentioned below

Services to Manufacturers

1. **Facilitating Large Scale Production** Wholesalers collect small orders from a number of retailers and pass on the pool of such orders to the manufacturers enabling them to produce on a large scale and take advantage of the economies of scale.
2. **Bearing Risk** The wholesale merchants bear variety of risks such as the risk of fall in prices, theft, pilferage, spoilage, fire, etc. and therefore, they relieve the manufacturers from bearing these risks.
3. **Financial Assistance** The wholesalers provide financial assistance to the manufacturers in the sense that they generally make cash payment for the goods purchased by them.
4. **Expert Advice** As the wholesalers are in direct contact with the retailers, they are in a position to advice the manufacturers about various aspects including customer's tastes and preferences, market conditions, competitive activities and the features preferred by the buyers.

5. **Help in Marketing Function** The wholesalers take care of the distribution of goods to a number of retailers. This relieves the manufacturers from many of the marketing activities and enables them to concentrate on the production activity.

6. **Facilitate Production Continuity** The wholesalers facilitate continuity of production activity throughout the year by purchasing the goods as and when these are produced and storing them till the time these are demanded by retailers or consumers in the market.

7. **Storage** Wholesalers reduce the burden of manufacturers of providing for storage facilities for the finished products by taking delivery of goods when these are produced in factory and keeping them in godowns/warehouses.

Services to Retailers

1. **Availability of Goods** The wholesalers make the products of various, manufacturers readily available to the retailers, relieving the retailers from the work of collecting goods from several producers.

2. **Marketing Support** The wholesalers perform various marketing functions and provide support to the retailers. They undertake advertising and other sales promotional activities to induce customers to purchase the goods.

3. **Grant of Credit** The wholesalers generally extend credit facilities to their regular customers which help retailers to manage their business with small amount of working capital.

4. **Specialised Knowledge** Wholesalers pass on the benefit of their specialised knowledge to the retailers by informing the retailers about the new products, their uses, quality, prices, etc.

5. **Risk Sharing** The wholesalers purchase in bulk and sell in small quantities to the retailers. Being able to purchase smaller quantities, retailers are in a position to avoid the risk of storage, theft, misuse, etc.

Retailers

Retail trade is performed by retailers. A retailer is engaged in the sale of goods and services directly to the ultimate consumers. Retailer represents the final stage in the distribution process.

A retailer offers various services to manufacturers/ wholesalers and consumers that are mentioned below

Services to Wholesalers/Manufacturers

1. **Help in Distribution of Goods** Retailers help in the distribution of their products by making them available to the final consumers, who may be scattered over a large geographic area.

2. **Personal Selling** By undertaking personal selling efforts, the retailers relieve the producers from this activity and greatly help them in the process of actualising the sale of the products.

3. **Enabling Large-scale Operations** On account of retailer's services, the manufacturers and wholesalers are freed from the trouble of making individual sales to consumers in small quantities.

4. **Collecting Market Information** As retailers remain in direct and constant touch with the buyers, they serve as an important source of collecting market information about the tastes, preferences and attitudes of customers.

5. **Help in Promotion** Retailers participate in promotional activities in various ways and thereby, help in promoting the sale of the products.

Services to Consumers

1. **Regular Availability of Products** The most important service of a retailer to consumers is to maintain regular availability of various products produced by different manufacturers.

2. **New Products Information** By arranging effective display of products, retailers provide important information about the arrival, special features, etc of new products to the customers.

3. **Convenience in Buying** Retailers generally buy goods in large quantities and sell these in small quantities, according to the requirements of their customers leading to great convenience to the customers.

4. **Wide Selection** Retailers generally keep stock of a variety of products of different manufacturers enabling the consumers to make their choice out of a wide selection of goods.

5. **After-sales Services** Retailers provide important after-sales services in the form of home delivery, supply of spare parts and attending complaints of customers.

6. **Provide Credit Facilities** The retailers sometimes provide credit facilities to their regular buyers.

Fixed Shop-Large Retailers

These retailers operate from a fixed shop on a very large scale. Their area of operation is wide. These are retail shops which maintain permanent establishment to sell their merchandise. Therefore, they do not move from place to place to serve their customers. They are of following types

Departmental Stores

It is a large establishment offering a wide variety of products, classified into well-defined departments. For example, there may be separate departments for toiletries, medicines, furniture, groceries, electronics, clothing and dress material within a store.

Features of Departmental Stores

- A modern departmental store may provide all facilities such as restaurant, travel and information bureau, telephone booth, restrooms, etc.

- These stores are generally located at a central place in the heart of a city.

- As the size of these stores is very large, they are generally formed as a joint stock company managed by a board of directors.
- A departmental store combines both the functions of retailing as well as warehousing.
- They have centralised purchasing arrangements. All the purchases in a department store are made centrally by the purchase department of the store.

Advantages of Departmental Stores

1. **Attract Large Number of Customers** As these stores are centrally located, they attract a large number of customers during the best part of the day.
2. **Convenience in Buying** By offering large variety of goods under one roof, the departmental stores provide great convenience to customers.
3. **Attractive Services** Some of the services offered by it include home delivery of goods, execution of telephone orders, grant of credit facilities and provision for restrooms, telephone booths, restaurants, saloons, etc.
4. **Economy of Large-scale Operations** As these stores are organised at a very large scale, these stores enjoy the benefits of large-scale operations.
5. **Promotion of Sales** The departmental stores are in a position to spend considerable amount of money on advertising and other promotional activities.

Limitations of Departmental Stores

1. **Lack of Personal Attention** It is very difficult to provide adequate personal attention to the customers in these stores.
2. **High Operating Cost** As these stores give more emphasis on providing services, their operating costs tend to be on the higher side.
3. **High Possibility of Loss** As a result of high operating costs and large scale operations, the chances of incurring losses in a departmental store are high.
4. **Inconvenient Location** As a departmental store is generally situated at a central location, it is not convenient for the purchase of goods that are needed at short notice.

Chain Stores or Multiple Shops

They are networks of retail shops that are owned and operated by manufacturers or intermediaries. A number of shops with similar appearance are established in localities and these shops normally deal in standardised and branded consumer products, which have rapid sales turnover. For example, an outlet of Reebok.

Features of Chain Stores

- These shops are located in fairly populous localities, where sufficient number of customers can be approached.
- The manufacturing/procurement of merchandise for all the retail units is centralised at the head office, from where the goods are despatched to each of these shops according to their requirements.
- Each retail shop is under the direct supervision of a branch manager, who is held responsible for its day-to-day management.
- All the branches are controlled by the head office, which is concerned with formulating the policies and getting them implemented.
- The prices of goods in such shops are fixed and all sales are made on cash basis.
- The head office normally appoints inspectors, who are concerned with day-to-day supervision of the shops, in respect of quality of customer service provided, adherence to the policies of the head office, etc.

Advantages of Chain Stores

1. **Economies of Scale** As there is central procurement, the multiple-shop organisation enjoys the economies of scale.
2. **Elimination of Middlemen** By selling directly to the consumers, the multiple-shop organisation is able to eliminate middlemen.
3. **No Bad Debts** Since all the sales in these shops are made on cash basis, there are no losses on account of bad debts.
4. **Transfer of Goods** The goods not in demand in a particular locality may be transferred to another locality where it is in demand.
5. **Diffusion of Risk** The losses incurred by one shop may be covered by profits in other shops.
6. **Low Cost** The multiple shops have lower cost of business due to centralised purchasing, elimination of middlemen and centralised promotion of sales.
7. **Flexibility** Under this system, if a shop is not operating at a profit, the management may decide to close it or shift it to some other place.

Limitations of Chain Stores

1. **Limited Selection of Goods** Some of the multiple shops deal only in limited range of products and not of other manufacturers.
2. **Lack of Initiative** The personnel do not take the initiative to use their creative skills to satisfy the customers as they are habitual of looking up to the head office for guidance.
3. **Lack of Personal Touch** Lack of initiative in the employees sometimes leads to indifference and lack of personal touch in them.
4. **Difficult to Change Demand** In case of sudden change of demand, the management may have to sustain huge losses because of large stocks lying unsold at the central depot.

Chapter Practice

Objective Questions

• Multiple Choice Questions

1. Basic objective of trade is
(a) social service
(b) profit
(c) environmental protection
(d) None of the above

Ans. (b) Trade refers to buying and selling of goods and it's basic objective is to earn profit.

2. Government levies taxes in order to generate funds to perform its various functions. Internal trade is liable to
(a) customs duty
(b) import duty
(c) GST
(d) export duty

Ans. (c) In internal trade, movement of goods and services is confined to the domestic territory of the nation. Therefore, customs duty, import duty and export duty is not leviable on them. GST (Goods and Service Tax) is an indirect tax levied in India on sale of goods and services within the domestic territory.

3. Wholesaler not just buys goods from manufacturers but they also help manufacturer in marketing of the product by
(a) storing goods in bulk quantities
(b) making cash payment
(c) transportation facilities
(d) conveying retailers' feedback to manufacturer

Ans. (d) The wholesalers are in direct contact with retailers. Therefore, they advise manufacturers about various aspects related to customers taste, preferences, market conditions, etc.

4. Wholesalers perform various ....functions which increases the demand of goods and ultimately increases the profits for retailers and manufacturers
(a) financing
(b) distribution
(c) marketing
(d) tax planning

Ans. (c) marketing

5. Time utility is being provided by ......
(a) retailers
(b) stockists
(c) wholesalers
(d) Both (a) and (c)

Ans. (c) Wholesalers keep the goods with themselves for a period of time till they are demanded by the retailers thereby creating a time utility.

6. **Statement I** No custom duty or import duty is levied on internal trade.
Statement II Storage facility provides with time utility.
Alternatives
(a) Statement I is correct and Statement II is wrong
(b) Statement II is correct and Statement I is wrong
(c) Both the statements are correct
(d) Both the statements are incorrect

Ans. (c) No custom duty or import duty is levied on internal trade as goods are part of domestic production and are meant for domestic consumption. Storage helps in bridging the gap between the time of production/procurement and the consumption of goods.

7. **Statement I** Wholesaler purchase in bulk quantity and sell in small lots to retailers.
Statement II The wholesalers perform various marketing functions and provide support to the consumer.
Alternatives
(a) Statement I is correct and Statement II is wrong
(b) Statement II is correct and Statement I is wrong
(c) Both the statements are correct
(d) Both the statements are incorrect

Ans. (a) The wholesalers perform various marketing functions and provide support to manufacturers and retailers.

8. Wholesaler provides financial assistance to manufacturers through
(a) bulk selling of goods to them
(b) loans
(c) purchase of goods in small quantities for cash
(d) bulk purchasing of goods in cash

Ans. (d) Manufacturers sell goods in bulk to wholesaler against cash payments. Therefore, it can be said that wholesalers provide financial assistance to manufacturers by bulk purchasing of goods against cash payments.

9. What types of service is not offered by retailers to manufacturers and wholesalers?
(a) New product information
(b) Personal selling
(c) Helps in promotion
(d) Helps in distribution of goods

Ans. (c)Helps in promotion

10. Retailers provide various services to the ultimate customers. One of such services is after sales service. Retailers provide after sale services to consumers in form of
(a) regular availability of goods
(b) credit facility
(c) wide selection
(d) home delivery

Ans. (d) Retailers usually have their place of business in a close proximity to the places where consumers live or market places. Due to this, they are able to provide important after sale services like home delivery of goods, supply of spare parts, mirror repairs or replacement, etc.

11. **Statement I** Departmental stores have a decentralised purchasing department, whereas sales are centralised in different departments.

Statement II Departmental stores can manage with less amount of capital.
Alternatives
(a) Statement I is correct and Statement II is wrong
(b) Statement II is correct and Statement I is wrong
(c) Both the statements are correct
(d) Both the statements are incorrect

Ans. (d) Departmental stores have a centralised purchasing department, whereas sales are decentralised in different departments. Departmental stores can manage with huge amount of capital.

12. Under which of the following areas, departmental stores are not at in advantageous position over smaller forms of retail businesses?
(a) Number of customers
(b) Operating costs
(c) Sales promotion
(d) Scale of operations

Ans. (b) Operating costs are high for departmental stores because they have to maintain the stores in a standardised manner and create different departments. They also have to hire high number of staff.

13. Which type of retail business acts as suppliers of a wide variety of products under one roof ?
(a) Departmental store
(b) Chain store
(c) Mail order houses
(d) Multiple shops

Ans. (a) Departmental store

14. In departmental stores, sales are ....according to different departments.
(a) unsegmented   (b) centralised
(c) decentralised   (d) None of these

Ans. (c) decentralised

15. **Statement I** Sales in chain stores are done on cash and credit basis.

Statement II Multiple shops normally deal in standardised and branded consumer products.
Alternatives
(a) Statement I is correct and Statement II is wrong
(b) Statement II is correct and Statement I is wrong
(c) Both the statements are correct
(d) Both the statements are incorrect

Ans. (b) Sales in chain stores are done on only cash basis.

16. Appollo Pharmacy has retail outlets running 24 hours a day and 7 days week. These retail outlets are spread across the country and have centralised purchasing and decentralised sales mechanism for sale of medicines and health care related goods to its customers. Which type of business outlet is highlighted in this paragraph?
(a) Departmental Store   (b) Chain store
(c) Both (a) and (b)   (d) None of these

Ans. (b) Chain store

17. Manufacturers sell goods directly through ...... and thus, eliminates unnecessary middlemen in the sale and purchase of goods.
(a) street vendors   (b) multi brand retail stores
(c) departmental stores   (d) chain stores

Ans. (d) chain stores

18. Each retail outlet (in chain stores setting) is under the direct supervision of a .... who is responsible for its day-to-day operations.
(a) head officer   (b) customer executive
(c) branch manager   (d) None of these

Ans. (c) branch manager

19. Which of following is/are the example(s) of chain stores?
(a) Bata showroom   (b) Dominos
(c) Raymond shop   (d) All of these

Ans. (d) All of these

20. Nature Beauty is a company with cosmetics stores all over the country. The procurement of raw materials and manufacturing of merchandise for all the retail units is centralised. Which type of store is highlighted here?
(a) Departmental Store   (b) Chain store
(c) Both (a) and (b)   (d) None of these

Ans. (b) Chain store

• Assertion-Reasoning MCQs

Directions (Q.Nos. 1-7) *There are two statements marked as Assertion (A) and Reason (R). Read the statements and choose the appropriate option from the options given below.*

    (a) Both Assertion (A) and Reason (R) are true and Reason (R) is the correct explanation of Assertion (A).

    (b) Both Assertion (A) and Reason (R) are true, but Reason (R) is not the correct explanation of Assertion (A).

    (c) Assertion (A) is true, but Reason (R) is false.

    (d) Assertion (A) is false, but Reason (R) is true.

1. Assertion (A) No custom duty or import duty is levied on internal trade.

    Reason (R) Goods involved in internal trade are part of domestic production and are meant for domestic consumption.

Ans. (a) Both Assertion (A) and Reason (R) are true and Reason (R) is the correct explanation of Assertion (A).

2. Assertion (A) Wholesalers bear risk which would have been borne by the retailers.

    Reason (R) The wholesale merchants deal in goods in their own name, take delivery of the goods and keep the goods purchased in large lots in their warehouses.

Ans. (d) In the process given in the reason, wholesalers bear risk which would have been borne by the manufacturers.

3. Assertion (A) Wholesalers inform the retailers about the new products, their uses, quality, prices, etc.

    Reason (R) The wholesalers specialise in one line of production.

Ans. (a) Both Assertion (A) and Reason (R) are true and Reason (R) is the correct explanation of Assertion (A).

4. Assertion (A) Retailers serve as an important source of collecting market information about the tastes, preferences and attitudes.

    Reason (R) Retailers are not in direct and constant touch with the buyers.

Ans. (c) Retailers remain in direct and constant touch with the buyers and therefore, serve as an important source of collecting market information about the tastes, preferences and attitudes.

5. Assertion (A) Retailers enable the consumers to make their choice.

    Reason (R) The retailers sometimes provide credit facilities to their regular buyers.

Ans. (b) Retailers generally keep stock of a variety of products. This enables the consumers to make their choice.

6. Assertion (A) It is convenient for customers to purchase goods from these departmental stores.

    Reason (R) Departmental stores offer a large variety of goods under one roof.

Ans. (a) Both Assertion (A) and Reason (R) are true and Reason (R) is the correct explanation of Assertion (A)

7. Assertion (A) Wholesalers relieve manufacturers from bearing multiple risks.

    Reason (R) The wholesalers provide cash payment to the manufacturers for the goods purchased.

Ans. (b) Wholesalers bear multiple risks of theft, pilferage, fire, change in process etc. and relieve the manufacturers from the same.

• Case Based MCQs

1. Direction *Read the following text and answer question no. (i) to (vi) on the basis of the same.*

Lavanya Cosmetics Ltd. located in Gujarat is a manufacturer of herbal cosmetic items and a leading enterprise in the industry. Its products are demanded all over the country. Seeing the increasing demand in October and November, their marketing and sales department has made a special herbal cosmetics gift hamper which is not only economic but has got a very attractive packing too.

For the distribution of such hampers at all places, they have made an agreement with Sharma traders who will buy from them such hampers in large quantities and will reach the products to retailers in every state so that they can meet their orders in time. In Gujarat, the company has opened its own retail outlet named 'Lavanya Stores' few months ago which is showing very good response of customers and increasing their sales turnover.

Inspired from the growth of sales of their retail store, they are having plans to open such stores in Rajasthan, Delhi and Punjab too. For testing the markets in these states, they decided to place the products in some big stores which offer a wide variety of products, classified into well-defined segments in the store.

With the success in these markets, the management decided to open more stores. They are planning to establish the system in such a way that the prices of the goods are fixed and sales are made on cash basis. Daily sales are to be deposited in a local bank account and details to this regard will be sent to the head office. However, the company faced an unprecedented problem that the employees working in these stores work on the instructions of the head office and do not stand to benefit in any way by the sales made by them. This affects their performance.

(i) Which of the following is incorrect regarding the services provided by wholesalers to manufacturers?
(a) Regular availability of products
(b) Help in marketing function
(c) Bearing risk
(d) Storage

Ans. (a) Regular availability of products

(ii) "In Gujarat the company has opened its own retail outlet, few months ago which is showing a very good response of customers and increasing their sales turnover.Inspired from the growth of sales of their retail store they are having plans to open such stores in Rajasthan, Delhi and Punjab too." Identify the type of fixed retail shop mentioned here.
(a) Market traders
(b) Multiple shops
(c) Departmental stores
(d) General store

Ans. (b) Multiple shops

(iii) "For the distribution of such hampers at all places, they have made an agreement with Sharma Traders." Which type of intermediary Sharma Traders is in internal trade?
(a) Wholesalers
(b) Retailers
(c) Commission agent
(d) Salesman

Ans. (a) Wholesalers

(iv) "They are planning to establish the system in such a way that the prices of the goods are fixed and sales are made on cash basis. Daily sales are to be deposited in a local bank account and details to this regard will be sent to the head office." Identify the feature of such stores.
(a) Central location
(b) Provision of services
(c) Centralised control
(d) Corporate status

Ans. (c) Centralised control

(v) "..... they decided to place the products in some big stores which offers a wide variety of products, classified into well-defined segments in the store." Which type of fixed shop is highlighted here?
(a) Chain stores
(b) Departmental stores
(c) Mail order houses
(d) Both (a) and (b)

Ans. (b) Departmental stores

(vi) Which problem of this kind of stores is highlighted in the lines, "the employees working in these stores work on the instructions of the head office and do not stand to benefit in any way by the sales made by them"?
(a) Lack of personal touch
(b) Lack of initiative
(c) Lack of personal attention
(d) High operating costs

Ans. (b) Lack of initiative

2. **Direction** *Read the following text and answer question no. (i) to (vi) on the basis of the same.*

Footwear Ltd. located in Mumbai manufactures shoes. It imports raw material from Italy and dyes from Japan. The design quality and durability of the shoes manufactured by this Company has made it number one company in that area. Now the company wishes to sell its products in all the states of India as well as in international markets.

The marketing managers advised to strengthen the distribution channel by appointing more wholesalers for each area. But one of the board of directors was of the view that if they sell the product directly to retailers, they will be able to get competitive price for their products, which will result in increased sales turnover and eventually the profits.

The promoters of the company have come up with a different proposition. They believe that the company should open its own stores in different parts of the country. After lot of discussion, it was decided to go ahead with the board of director's proposal that they should sell the products directly to retailers. They also believe that retailers will provide important information about the arrival of products to the customers by arranging effective display of products.

(i) ...... serves as the link between wholesalers and customers.
(a) Suppliers   (b) Retailers
(c) Manufactures   (d) All of these

Ans. (b) Retailers

(ii) Which of the following is incorrect regarding the services provided by retailers to consumers?
(a) Provide after sales services
(b) Offer wide selection of goods
(c) Provide credit facilities to regular buyers
(d) None of the above

Ans. (d) None of the above

(iii) Trade is an important function of
(a) wholesalers   (b) retailers
(c) manufactures
(d) Both wholesalers and retailers

Ans. (d) Both wholesalers and retailers

(iv) Which of the following statements regarding reasons for international business are correct?
   (a) Unequal distribution of natural resources among nations or differences in their productivity levels
   (b) Availability of various factors of production differs among nations
   (c) Labour productivity and production costs differ among nations due to various socio-economic, geographical and political reasons
   (d) All of the above

Ans. (d) All of the above

 (v) Which of the following is the proposition of the promoters?
   (a) Mail order houses   (b) Chain stores
   (c) Departmental stores   (d) None of these

Ans. (b) Chain stores

(vi) Which service to customer by retailer is highlighted in the line, "They also believe that retailers will provide important information about the arrival of products to the customers by arranging effective display of products."?
   (a) Regular availability of products
   (b) New products information
   (c) Convenience in buying
   (d) Wide selection

Ans. (b) New products information

3. Direction *Read the following text and answer question no. (i) to (vi) on the basis of the same.*

John, Brad and Simon are three friends who wants to start a business of trading and manufacturing high quality herbal products. They have been trying to figure out the right mode of running the business by evaluating each and every option.

John thinks that they should place the products in big stores where there is already a cosmetics section so that customers can easily find the product.

Simon is of the different view who believes that they should open their own stores in different cities and localities so that they develop a unique brand image.

He gives the argument that if a store is incurring loss, then it can be closed down or shifted to some other place, without any significant effect on the company.

However, Brad produces counter-argument by saying that due to operating on a large scale and lack of initiative on the part of employees, their dealings with customers will lack personal touch. Therefore, he suggested that they should deliver the goods at home with a personalised note. They decided to further explore the options.

They decided that they will go with the option that Simon suggested. They also set up retail chain with many mom-and-pop stores. They believe that these stores will help them in creating place utility. Moreover, these stores will tell the consumers about their products helping them to boost sales.

 (i) Which fixed-shop large retailer John highlighted?
   (a) Departmental stores
   (b) Chain stores
   (c) Mail order houses
   (d) None of the above

Ans. (a) Departmental stores

 (ii) Which fixed-shop large retailer Simon highlighted?
   (a) Departmental stores   (b) Chain stores
   (c) Mail order houses   (d) None of these

Ans. (b) Chain stores

(iii) Which merit of a particular business type was highlighted by Simon?
   (a) No bad debts   (b) Low cost
   (c) Flexibility   (d) Economies of scale

Ans. (c) Flexibility

(iv) Which demerit of a particular business type was highlighted by Brad?
   (a) Lack of initiative
   (b) Lack of personal touch
   (c) Loss due to change in demand
   (d) Limited selection of goods

Ans. (b) Lack of personal touch

 (v) Which service of retailers to manufacturers is highlighted in the line, "They also set up retail chain with many mom-and-pop stores. They believe that these stores will help them in creating place utility."?
   (a) Help in distribution of goods
   (b) Personal selling
   (c) Enabling large-scale operations
   (d) Help in promotion

Ans. (a) Help in distribution of goods

(vi) Which service of retailers to consumers is highlighted in the line, "Moreover, these stores will tell the consumers about their products helping them to boost sales."?
   (a) Regular availability of products
   (b) New products information
   (c) Convenience in buying
   (d) Wide selection

Ans. (b) New products information

PART 2
Subjective Questions

• Short Answer (SA) Type Questions

1. What do you mean by trade? Also explain its classification.

Ans. Trade refers to buying and selling of goods and services with the objective of earning profit. It bridges the gap between the producer and the consumer.

Trade can broadly be classified into two categories

(i) **Internal Trade** Trade which takes place within a country is called internal trade.

(ii) **External Trade** Trade which takes place between two or more countries is called external trade.

2. Explain the concept of internal trade along with its key features. **(NCERT)**

Ans. When buying and selling of goods and services take place within a country, it is referred to as internal trade.

Some of the important features of internal trade are

(i) All payments are made in the national currency.

(ii) Generally, there are no restrictions on the movements of goods.

(iii) Several alternative modes of transport are available for carrying goods.

3. Wholesalers serve two-way purpose by providing warehousing facilities. Comment. **(NCERT)**

Ans. Two-way purpose is served by wholesalers by providing warehousing facilities in the following manner

(i) Wholesalers take delivery of goods when these are produced in factory and keep them in their godowns/warehouses, which reduces the burden on manufacturers for providing storage facilities for the finished products.

(ii) Warehousing by wholesalers relieves the retailers of the work of collecting goods from several producers and keeping huge inventory of the same.

4. Shyam started a hosiery factory with just 4 workers to manufacture ladies wear. The firm tasted success in business and installed new machines and hired more workers and engaged supervisors. Though his business was expanding, he was able to manage the marketing part of the business. He sold directly to customers and also to retailers in his city. About 6 months back, Shyam admitted two partners into the business to expand the business further. Both the partners contributed capital of ₹ 40 lakh each. Fresh funds were used to acquire advanced machines and purchase raw materials and other inputs. The production has increased 5 times but difficulties are being faced in marketing of finished products.

The new partners want appointment of wholesalers to distribute the products though Shyam is not in favour of this idea.

(i) What marketing options are available with the firm?

(ii) Should wholesalers be appointed to sell the products? Why?

Ans. The options available with the firm are

(i) The firms may open its own sale outlets in different parts of the city to sell its products. The firm may appoint wholesalers and retailers for the distribution of its products.

(ii) In this case, it is advisable to appoint wholesalers because of the following reasons

(a) The firm does not have enough capital to open new stores and even the firm does not have capability to raise funds.

(b) By appointing wholesalers, the firm would be relieved of the botheration of marketing its products.

(c) Though wholesalers take away a part of the profits margin, they provide useful services in return. These services are

• They sell goods to retailers and big customers.

• They can arrange for advertisement of goods and display of goods at retail outlets.

In nutshell, the wholesalers would provide specialised services to market the products. This would allow the firm to concentrate on increasing production and also quality.

5. A very successful Ayurveda Company of the country sells its products to distributors who sell the products to wholesalers as and when demand is generated. These wholesalers demand the products from distributors depending upon the market demand and trends. The company contacts doctors of the country who prescribes the ayurvedic medicines to the patients. These patients demand the medicines from chemists who in turn ask the wholesalers to supply them the medicines. Identify and explain two types of internal trade highlighted in the above passage. Also, quote the lines to substantiate the answers.

Ans. (i) **Wholesale Trade** "These wholesalers demand the products from distributors depending upon the market demand and trends."

Wholesale trade refers to purchasing goods and services in large quantity from manufacturers (or distributors of manufacturers) and reselling them to retailers, who then sells them to the ultimate consumers. A wholesaler is an intermediary between manufacturer and retailer.

Chain of Wholesale Trade

Manufacturers —— Wholesalers —- Retailers —- Consumers

(ii) **Retail Trade** "….from chemists who in turn ask the wholesalers to supply them the medicines."

Retail trade refers to purchasing relatively small quantity of goods from wholesalers and selling them to ultimate consumers. A retailer is an intermediary between wholesaler and consumer.

Chain of Retail Trade

Wholesalers —- Retailers —- Consumers

6. Bhargav Enterprises (BE) is a wholesaler outlet in East Delhi. This outlet deals with products from personal care segment ranging from perfumes to talcum powders to shaving creams, so on and so forth. BE advertises the product through banners and activities in nearby areas to increase the demand of the products.

Since the outlet is in operations for many years now, it has cordial relations with retailers and therefore, the trusted outlets are not billed on immediate cash basis which helped them to work with low capital. In the process, it not only helps them to avoid financial burden but also helps them in avoiding the risk of theft and storage as retailers can demand good in smaller quantities. BE also keeps the retailers updated with the new products launched in the market.

Identify and explain the services given by the wholesalers to the retailers by quoting the lines.

Ans. Services given by the wholesalers to retailers in the given case are

(i) **Marketing Support** "BE advertises the product through banners and activities in nearby areas to increase the demand of the products."

The wholesalers perform various marketing functions such as advertisements and other sales promotional activities to induce customers to purchase the goods. This increases the demand of the products which results in increased profits for the retailer.

(ii) **Grant of Credit** " …..and therefore, the trusted outlets are not billed on immediate cash basis which helped them to work with low capital."

The wholesalers generally extend credit facilities to retailers. This enables them to manage their business with relatively small amount of working capital.

(iii) **Specialised Knowledge** "BE also keeps the retailers updated with the new products launched in the market."

The wholesalers specialise in one line of production. They inform the retailers about the new products, their uses, quality, prices, etc.

(iv) **Risk Sharing** "In the process, it not only helps them to avoid financial burden but also helps them in avoiding the risk of theft and storage as retailers can demand good in smaller quantities."

The wholesalers purchase in bulk and sell in small quantities to the retailers. Being able to purchase smaller quantities, retailers are in a position to avoid the risk of storage, theft, misuse, etc.

7. What difficulties would a consumer face if there is no retail shop?

Ans. A consumer would face following difficulties if there is no retail shop (any three points)

(i) In the absence of a retail shop, consumer will have to store the goods.

(ii) In the absence of a retail shop, a consumer shall not be able to make a good selection.

(iii) A retail shop supplies goods in the quantities which suit the pocket and needs of different consumers. In the absence of a retail shop, a consumer will have to approach a wholesaler or a manufacturer and buy the goods in large quantities.

(iv) There will be lot of inconvenience to the consumers.

(v) Consumers will not be able to know about the new products available in the market.

8. What are the services offered by retailers to wholesalers?

Ans. Retailers render following services to the wholesalers

(i) **Help in Distribution of Goods** Retailers provide help in the distribution of goods and making them available to final consumers.

(ii) **Personal Selling** The retailers relieve the producers from selling the goods personally and help them in actualising the sale of the products.

(iii) **Enabling Large Scale Operations** It enables them to operate on a large scale and fully concentrate on production activities.

(iv) **Collecting Market Information** Retailers remain in touch with the buyers. They know about the tastes, attitudes, preference, etc. Such information is very useful in taking marketing decisions in an organisation.

9. Goel and sons is a grocer based in Meerut, UP. It is an outlet retailing daily day to day ration and other branded products. They have been in business for last 20 years and therefore, have developed good reputation in the market. They provide information about the arrival, special features, etc of products to the customers and sell goods in small quantities, according to the requirements of these customers. They also have a special scheme where they supply good to the home within certain range of area on a purchase of some minimum amount of goods. On the basis of loyalty of customers, they sometimes sell goods to the regular customers on purchase now, pay later basis.

The above case highlights some of the services retailer provides to the consumers. Identify and explain these services by quoting the lines.

Ans. Services provided by retailers to customers are

(i) **New Products Information** "They provide information about the arrival, special features, etc of products to the customers...."

By arranging effective display of products, retailers provide important information about the arrival, special features, etc of products to the customers.

(ii) **Convenience in Buying** "..... sell goods in small quantities, according to the requirements of these customers."

Retailers generally sell goods in small quantities, according to the requirements of their customers. This offers great convenience to the customers.

(iii) **After Sales Services** "They also have a special scheme where they supply good to the home within certain range of area on a purchase of some minimum amount of goods."

Retailers provide important after-sales services in the form of home delivery, supply of spare parts etc.

(iv) **Provide Credit Facilities** "On the basis of loyalty of customers, they sometimes sell goods to the regular customers on purchase now, pay later basis."

The retailers sometimes provide credit facilities to their regular buyers, leading to increased level of consumption and better standard of living.

10. Differentiate between retailers and wholesalers on following basis

(i) Purchases and sales   (ii) Quantity of goods
(iii) Specialisation   (iv) Capital

Ans. The differences between wholesalers and retailers are

Basis	Wholesalers	Retailers
Purchases and Sales	They purchase goods from manufacturers and sell them to retailers.	They purchase goods from wholesalers and sell them to ultimate consumers.
Quantity of Goods	They buy and sell goods in large quantities.	They buy and sell goods in small quantities.
Specialisation	They specialise, generally, in purchase and sale of one commodity only.	They do not specialise in only one good, but provide all types of goods.
Capital	They require a large amount of capital.	They require comparatively less capital.

11. Explain some of the major features of departmental stores.

Ans. Some of the important features of a departmental store are

(i) A modern departmental store may provide all facilities such as restaurant, restrooms, etc. In this way, they try to provide maximum service to higher class of customers, for whom price is of secondary importance.

(ii) These stores are generally located at a central place in the city, which caters to a large number of customers.

(iii) They are generally formed as a joint stock company, managed by a board of directors as the size of these stores is very large.

(iv) A departmental store combines both the functions of retailing as well as warehousing. They purchase directly from manufacturers and operate separate warehouses, thereby eliminating undesirable middlemen between the producers and the customers for their products.

12. 'Easy Day' , 'Vishal Mega Mart' and 'Big Bazaar' are the examples of which type of fixed shops? Give any two merits.

Ans. 'Easy Day', 'Vishal Mega Mart' and 'Big Bazaar' are the examples of departmental stores.

Merits of departmental stores are

(i) A departmental store keeps very wide variety of goods with different designs, colours, styles, etc.

(ii) Departmental stores provide various types of services to customers. They extend liberal credit, accept telephone order, provide for free home delivery services, etc.

13. Multiple shops are networks of retail shops that are owned and operated by manufacturers or intermediaries. Under this type of arrangement, a number of shops with similar appearance are established in localities, spread over different parts of the country. These shops normally deal in standardised and branded consumer products, which have rapid sales turnover. In the light of the statement, state any four features of multiple shops.

Ans. Features of multiple shops are (any four)

(i) These shops are located in populous localities, so that customers can be served at a place near their residence.

(ii) The manufacturing or procurement of merchandise for all the retail units is centralised.

(iii) Each retail outlet is under the direct supervision of a branch manager, who is responsible for its day-to-day operations.

(iv) All branches are controlled by the head office. The head office formulates policies and gets them implemented.

(v) The price of the goods is fixed and sales are made on cash basis. Daily sales are deposited in a local bank account and details to this regard are sent to the head office.

14. Zar is a company who have got stores all around the country. They are famous for quality clothes which are supplied at a not so expensive price. The clothes are also said to be very fashionable and are always in trend in the urban youth and working class. However, they only sell clothes manufactured by them and not of any other company. These stores work on the instructions of head office and have little to no motivation to sell effectively.

The customers usually choose clothes themselves and at times, no salesperson is involved leaving the customers all by themselves. At times, the company burns its clothes when demand trend changes rapidly and company's large stock remains unsold. The above case highlights some of the disadvantages of chain stores. Identify and explain these by quoting the lines.

Ans. Disadvantages of chain stores highlighted in the case are

(i) **Limited Selection of Goods** "However, they only sell clothes manufactured by them and not of any other company."

Majority of the multiple shops deal only in limited range of products. For example, Reebok deals in sportswear and foot wear. These stores do not sell products of other manufacturers. Therefore, customers visiting these stores have only selected items to choose from.

(ii) **Lack of Initiative** "These stores work on the instructions of head office and have little to no motivation to sell effectively."

The employees working in these stores work on the instructions of the head office. Also, they do not stand to benefit in any way by the sales made by them. So, they do not take initiative on their own.

(iii) **Lack of Personal Touch** "The customers usually choose clothes themselves and at times, no salesperson is involved leaving the customers all by themselves."

Due to operating on a large scale and lack of initiative on the part of employees, their dealings with customers lack personal touch.

(iv) **Loss Due to Change in Demand** "At times, the company burns its clothes when demand trend changes rapidly and company's large stock remains unsold."

If the demand for the goods sold by these stores change rapidly, then the management may have to sustain heavy losses, because of large stocks lying unsold at the central depot.

• Long Answer (LA) Type Questions

1. Wholesalers play an inevitable role in the success of the manufacturers of various goods. Comment on this statement by stating the services provided by the wholesalers to manufacturers.

Ans. The services provided by the wholesalers to manufacturers are (any six)

(i) **Facilitating Large Scale Production** Wholesalers collect small orders from a number of retailers and pass on the pool of such orders to the manufacturers and make purchases in bulk quantities. This enables the producers to undertake production on a large scale.

(ii) **Bearing Risk** The wholesale merchants deal in goods in their own name, take delivery of the goods and keep the goods purchased in large lots in their warehouses. In this process, they bear risk which would have been borne by the manufacturer.

(iii) **Financial Assistance** They provide financial assistance to the manufacturers as they generally make cash payment for the goods purchased by them.

(iv) **Expert Advice** The wholesalers are in direct contact with the retailers, therefore they can advice the manufacturers about various aspects related to customer's tastes and preferences, market conditions, etc.

(v) **Help in the Marketing Function** The wholesalers distribute goods to a number of retailers. They in turn, sell to a large number of customers thus, helping to market the product.

(vi) **Facilitates Continuity** The wholesalers facilitate continuity of production activity throughout the year by purchasing the goods as and when they are produced.

(vii) **Storage** Wholesalers take delivery of goods when they are produced and keep them in their godowns/warehouses, thereby helping in storage of goods.

2. Explain any four advantages of departmental stores.

Ans. The advantages of departmental stores are (any four)

(i) **Attract Large Number of Customers** As these stores are centrally located, therefore they attract a large number of customers.

(ii) **Convenience in Buying** These stores offer a large variety of goods under one roof. Therefore, it is convenient for customers to purchase goods from these stores.

(iii) **Attractive Services** These stores provide extra services to the customers, such as, home delivery of goods, accepting orders through telephone and online, provision of rest rooms, restaurants, etc.

    (iv) **Economy of Large-scale Operations** These stores are organised and managed on a large scale. Therefore, they are able to enjoy economies of large scale operations and increase their profits.

    (v) **Promotion of Sales** The departmental stores are in a position to spend considerable amount of money on advertising and other promotional activities which help in boosting the sales.

3. Akbarally was the first departmental store of India. There were two full line department stores and eight supermarkets called Mini-Akbarallys across Mumbai. This store was generating phenomenal profits upto 1990s, but with the onset of the retail boom in 1990s and the subsequent proliferation of speciality stores, malls and branded stores, the downward slide of Akbarally began. In 2009, not being able to sustain losses, Akbarally closed down.

  (i) What are departmental stores?

  (ii) State the limitations of departmental stores which could have been the cause of Akbarally's failure.

Ans. (i) Departmental store is a large establishment offering a wide variety of products, classified into well-defined departments. A departmental store aims at satisfying practically all the needs of the consumers under one roof. It has a number of departments, each one confining its activities to a specific kind of product.

  (ii) Following are the limitations of departmental stores which could have been the cause of Akbarally's failure

    (a) **Lack of Personal Attention** Because of large scale operations, these stores are not able to give personal attention to each and every customer.

    (b) **High Operating Costs** Since these stores provide a number of additional services to their customers, therefore their operating costs are also high.

    (c) **High Possibility of Loss** These stores operate on large scale and incur high operating costs. Therefore, their exposure to risk is also high.

    (d) **Inconvenient Location** These stores are generally located in a central location. Customers encounter traffic problems while visiting these stores. Also, it is not convenient for the purchase of goods that are needed at short notice.

4. Chain stores have some inherent advantages. Comment.

Ans. Chain stores exhibits following advantages (any six)

  (i) **Economies of Scale** These stores operate on a high scale and procure the goods centrally. Therefore, they are also able to enjoy economies of scale.

  (ii) **Elimination of Middlemen** Through these stores, the manufacturers sell goods directly to the consumers, thus eliminating unnecessary middlemen in the sale and purchase of goods.

  (iii) **No Bad Debts** All the sales in these stores are made on cash. Therefore, there is no question of bad debts.

  (iv) **Transfer of Goods** In case of lack of demand, goods from one store can be transferred to another store.

  (v) **Diffusion of Risk** The risk is spread over a number of shops. Loss from one shop can be recovered from the profit of another shop.

  (vi) **Low Cost** Because of centralised purchasing, elimination of middlemen and centralised promotion of sales, chain stores have low operational costs.

  (vii) **Flexibility** This system offers the advantage of flexible operations. If a shop is incurring loss, then it can be closed down or shifted to some other place, without any significant effect on the organisation.

5. Pad Chihan Limited is a large-sized company manufacturing shoes. It has to determine whether it should use wholesalers or set up its own chain stores for distributing its products. What alternatives would you suggest? Give reasons in support of your answer.

Ans. In the above case, we find there are two alternatives before the company

  (i) To have wholesalers as middlemen.   (ii) have its own multiple shops

Both the alternatives have their own merits and demerits. We suggest multiple shops are the better alternative than the wholesalers due to following reasons

  (i) Multiple shops eliminate middlemen. Hence, there is direct contact between the company and consumers. All advantages of elimination of wholesalers can be enjoyed.

  (ii) Since the company is large sized, it means company has sufficient financial resources to have its own shops. Thus, the company is in a position to eliminate middlemen.

  (iii) Company is manufacturing shoes i.e., durable consumer product, therefore, multiple shops are better alternative.

  (iv) Company can approach maximum customers through its own shops. Wholesalers may not find it profitable to deal in shoes of a new company and therefore, wholesalers will not be taking interest.

  (v) Multiple shops have a better appeal to consumers. Bata Shoe Company is a good example.

    In brief, we can suggest to the company that multiple shops will be the better alternative for distribution of its product-shoes.

6. Differentiate between departmental stores and chain stores/multiple shops.

Ans. The differences between departmental stores and chain stores are

Basis	Departmental Stores	Chain Stores
Location	A departmental store is located at a central place, where a large number of customers can be attracted.	A chain store is located at a number of places within a approach of a large number of customers. Thus, central location is not necessary for a chain store.
Range of Products	Departmental stores aim at satisfying all the needs of customers under one roof. As such, they have to maintain a variety of products of different types.	Chain stores aim to satisfy the requirements of customers relating to a specified range of products only.
Services Offered	The departmental stores lay great emphasis on providing maximum service to their customers. Some of the services, provided by them include free wi-fi, restaurant and so on.	Chain stores provide very limited service confined to guarantees and repairs if the sold out goods turn out to be defective.
Pricing	The departmental stores, however, do not have uniform pricing policy for all the departments; rather they have to occasionally offer discounts on certain products and varieties to clear their stock.	Chain stores sell goods at fixed prices and maintain uniform pricing policies for all the shops.
Class of Customers	The departmental stores cater to the needs of relatively high income group of customers, who care more for the services provided rather than the prices of the product.	Chain stores cater to different types of customers, including those belonging to the lower income groups, who are interested in buying quality goods at reasonable prices.
Credit Facilities	Departmental stores may provide credit facilities to some of their regular customers.	All sales in the chain stores are made strictly on cash basis.

Chapter Test

Multiple Choice Questions

1. Which of the following is not a service offered by wholesaler to manufacturer?
   (a) Storage   (b) Grant of credit   (c) Bearing risk   (d) Financial assistance

2. All the branches of chain stores are controlled by
   (a) branches themselves   (b) head office
   (c) city office   (d) general manager of each branch

3. In chain store, the ...... manager sends daily reports to the head office.
   (a) city   (b) area   (c) branch   (d) region

4. Retailer is at the end of the distribution chain. Based on the demand from the consumers, retailers buy goods of different types from various wholesalers and make them available to final consumers. By doing so retailers create
   (a) place utility   (b) time utility   (c) profit utility   (d) price utility

5. Statement I Departmental stores give high level of personal attention to all the customers.
   Statement II Departmental stores are generally located in central locations.
   Alternatives
   (a) Statement I is correct and Statement II is wrong   (b) Statement II is correct and Statement I is wrong
   (c) Both the statements are correct   (d) Both the statements are incorrect

Short Answer (SA) Type Questions

1. State any three important features of Internal trade.

2. Discuss the features of a departmental store which makes it different from other stores.

3. Differentiate between departmental stores and chain stores on following basis.
   (i) Services offered   (ii) Pricing   (iii) Class of customers   (iv) Credit facilities

4. Mention the various features of chain stores.

5. Reekob is a shoe brand operating in the world. It has got stores all over the country with wide variety of footwears. The footwears of Reekob are known to be of premium quality and therefore, attract upper-middle-income and upper-income segment of the society. The company manufactures these footwears and sells them directly through the stores. The stores also have the policy that when certain SKUs are not available in one store, they are transferred by the other store. The company remains fairly with positive cash flow as some or the other stores are generating good profits for the company. Identify and explain the advantages of the chain stores by quoting the lines.

Long Answer (LA) Type Questions

1. KKK is a departmental store in the city of Mumbai. The store has 5 different sections for five different items Food & Beverages, books & accessories, personal care, health care and kids' zone. Because of multiple sections, it experiences a large footfall during all the working hours. Store has the facility of home delivery and even accepts the orders in the online mode. But because of all these services and facilities, it has got very high operational cost due to which the profits are hampered. However, it has always been compensated by good foot fall but recently it has faced decrease in number of people coming in. Fortunately, the departmental store is in a position to spend considerable amount of money on advertising and other promotional activities to boost the sales. But this comes with a slight factor that due to large footfall, the store is not able to give personal attention to each and every customer. So to improve the services, they decided to take feedback from the customers through a feedback form. In the time, it was reflected by the customers that they would like a parking facility near the store because the store is located in an area of heavy traffic which makes it difficult for them to park on the roadside.

   The passage above highlights some of the advantages and disadvantages of departmental stores. Identify three advantages and three disadvantages each by quoting the lines.

2. Wholesalers not only provide services to the retailers but also to the manufacturers. In the light of the statement, explain the services provided by the wholesalers to the manufacturers.

Answers

Multiple Choice Questions

   1. (b)   *2. (b)*   *3. (c)*   *4. (a)*   *5. (b)*

For Detailed Solutions
Scan the code

CHAPTER 04

International Business

In this Chapter...

- Meaning of International Business
- Advantages of International Business

Meaning of International Business

Manufacturing and trading beyond the boundaries of one's own country is known as international business. It can be defined as those business activities that take place across the national frontiers. It involves not only the international movement of goods and services, but also of capital, personnel, technology and intellectual property like patents, trademarks, copyright, etc.

International trade is the component of international business. It comprises of buying and selling of goods and services beyond the geographical borders of the country. It is also referred to as 'foreign trade' or 'external trade'. It can also be understood as exchange of goods and services between residents of different countries. It involves the use of foreign exchange to discharge trade obligations.

Reasons for International Business

Following are the for internatinal business

1. **Uneven Distribution of Natural Resources** All the countries cannot produce equally or cheaply becauses of uneven distribution of natural resources among them as well as differences in their productivity levels. Thus, contries exchange their surplus production with goods that they are in short supply in their country.
2. **Factors of Production Availability** Each country differ in terms of availability of various factors of production such as labour, capital and raw materials, needed for producing different goods and services.
3. **Specialisation of Products** Many countries specialise in the production of certain goods and services for which they have some advantages such as suitable climatic conditions, technical know how, high labour productivity, etc.
4. **Benefits of Cost** Cost of production differ in different countries due to different socio-economic, political and geographical conditions. Many of the countries are in a better position to produce some goods more economically than other countries. Thus, companies engage in international business so as to import available resources from other countries at lower prices and export goods on which they can fetch better prices.

Advantages of International Business

International business is advantageous to both nations as well as business firms.

Advantages to Nations

1. **Earning of Foreign Exchange** International business helps countries to earn foreign exchange. This helps a country to import capital goods, technology, petroleum products and fertilizers, pharmaceutical products and other consumer products which otherwise might not be available domestically.

2. **More Efficient Use of Resources** Since, countries tend to produce goods in which they have a comparative advantage, wasteful duplication of resources is prevented and they end up producing more. Thus, countries export surplus production of such goods to import those goods in which other countries have specialisation. It facilitates more efficient and optimum use of resources.

3. **Improving Growth Prospects and Employment Potential** International business improves the growth prospects of many countries, especially the developing ones as firms can raise their production capacity and export surplus output to foreign countries. Also, many countries follow the principle 'export and flourish' and improve their growth prospects, thereby, creating employment opportunities for their citizens.

4. **Increased Standard of Living** International business helps people of a country to have access to a large variety of goods and services. This helps them to improve their standard of living.

Advantages to Firms

1. **Prospects for Higher Profits** When prices in the domestic market are low, firms can earn more profits by selling their products in those countries in which prices are high.

2. **Increased Capacity Utilisation** Many business and industrial enterprises have unused capacity, that can be efficiently utilised for further production. Thus, surplus production can be used to generate extra profits from foreign trade.

3. **Prospects for Growth** When the domestic demand for a firm's product or service start getting saturated in the domestic market, then firms can considerably improve prospects of their growth by venturing out in the international market.

4. **Way Out to Intense Competition in Domestic Market** Highly competitive domestic market drives many companies to go international in search of markets for their products.

5. **Improved Business Vision** Most enterprises have an urge to grow, to become more competitive, to diversify and derive the benefits of going global through international trade.

Difference between Domestic and International Business

Basis	Domestic Business	International Business
Nationality of Buyers and Sellers	People or organisations from one nation participate in domestic business transactions.	People or organisations of different countries participate in international business transactions.
Nationality of Other Stakeholders	Various other stakeholders such as suppliers, employees, middlemen, shareholders and partners are usually citizens of the same country.	Various other stakeholders such as suppliers, employees, middlemen, shareholders and partners are from different nations.
Mobility of Factors of Production	The degree of mobility of factors of production like labour and capital is relatively more within a country.	The degree of mobility of factors of production like labour and capital across nations is relatively less.
Customer Heterogeneity across Markets	Domestic markets are relatively more homogeneous in nature.	International markets lack homogeneity due to differences in language, preferences, customs, etc., across markets.
Differences in Business Systems and Practices	Business systems and practices are relatively more homogeneous within a country.	Business systems and practices vary considerably across countries.
Political System and Risks	Domestic business is subject to political system and risks of one single country.	Different countries have different forms of political systems and different degrees of risks which often become a barrier to international business.
Business Regulations and Policies	Domestic business is subject to rules, laws and policies, taxation system, etc., of a single country.	International business transactions are subject to rules, laws and policies, tariffs and quotas, etc. of multiple countries.
Currency used in Business Transactions	Currency of domestic country is used.	International business transactions involve use of currencies of more than one country.

Chapter Practice

Objective Questions

• Multiple Choice Questions

1. The basic problem faced by those engaged in international trade is 'different countries have different currencies'. In order to resolve this issue, which currency is considered as the most popular currency in international trade?
(a) US Dollars
(b) UK Euro
(c) Japanese Yen
(d) Indian Rupee

Ans. (a) US Dollars

2. International trade requires movement of goods across the boundaries of a nation. Which of the following is the cheapest mode of transporting goods to longer distances?
(a) Road
(b) Rail
(c) Ships
(d) Air

Ans. (c) Ships

3. International business involves .... degree of risk.
(a) low
(b) moderate
(c) high
(d) Can't be determined

Ans. (c) high

4. In case of international business, there is a wide time gap between order and ..... of goods.
(a) demand
(b) supply
(c) trade
(d) exchange

Ans. (b) supply

5. The fundamental reason behind international business is that the countries cannot produce all the goods that they need, with respect to
(a) quality
(b) cost
(c) Both (a) and (b)
(d) None of these

Ans. (c) Both (a) and (b)

6. Cost of production differ in different countries due to .... factor.
(a) Socio-economic
(b) Political
(c) Geographical
(d) All of these

Ans. (d) All of these

7. Labour, capital and .... are the factors of production whose availability differs from country to country.
(a) Tools
(b) Entrepreneurs
(c) Raw material
(d) All of these

Ans. (c) Raw material

8. Which type of domestic markets drive companies to go international in search of new markets for their products?
(a) Monopolistic markets
(b) Highly competitive markets
(c) Oligopoly
(d) Monopoly

Ans. (b) Due to highly competitive domestic market, there is not much of a scope left for growth in the domestic market. Therefore, many companies tend to go international in search of new markets for their products.

9. International trade should be done with extreme caution as it may lead to ...... use of natural resources, which may make a country poor by depleting its natural resources.
(a) extensive
(b) intensive
(c) moderate
(d) regressive

Ans. (b) International trade may make nations greedy for growth and development which may cause them to use their natural resources intensively. This makes nations poor in the long run by depleting its natural resources.

10. International trade has its own advantages and disadvantages. Which of the following is not an area which puts international trade at disadvantageous position?
(a) Language
(b) Time involved
(c) Intensive use of natural resources
(d) Capacity utilisation

Ans. (d) Capacity utilisation

11. International trade is advantageous to
(a) nations   (b) firms
(c) Both (a) and (b)   (d) None of these
Ans. (c) Both (a) and (b)

12. Which of these is an advantage of international business to the nation?
(a) Better Utilisation of Resources
(b) Prospects for Higher Profits
(c) Way Out to Intense Competition in Domestic Market
(d) All of these
Ans. (a) Better Utilisation of Resources

13. **Statement I** The degree of mobility of factors of production like labour and capital across nations is relatively less.

Statement II Domestic markets are relatively less homogeneous in nature as compared to international markets.
Alternatives
(a) Statement I is correct and Statement II is wrong
(b) Statement II is correct and Statement I is wrong
(c) Both the statements are correct
(d) Both the statements are incorrect
Ans. (a) Domestic markets are relatively more homogeneous in nature as compared to international markets.

14. **Statement I** In international business, there is use of domestic currency.

Statement II Business systems and practices vary considerably across countries.
Alternatives
(a) Statement I is correct and Statement II is wrong
(b) Statement II is correct and Statement I is wrong
(c) Both the statements are correct
(d) Both the statements are incorrect
Ans. (b) In international business, there is use of foreign currencies.

15. **Statement I** A large number of domestic firms in India found it very difficult to compete in the world market.

Statement II In International business, various other stakeholders such as suppliers, employees, middlemen, shareholders and partners are from different nations.
Alternatives
(a) Statement I is correct and Statement II is wrong
(b) Statement II is correct and Statement I is wrong
(c) Both the statements are correct
(d) Both the statements are incorrect
Ans. (c) Both the statements are correct

• Assertion–Reasoning MCQs

Directions (Q.Nos. 1-3) *There are two statements marked as Assertion (A) and Reason (R). Read the statements and choose the appropriate option from the options given below.*
(a) Both Assertion (A) and Reason (R) are true and Reason (R) is the correct explanation of Assertion (A).
(b) Both Assertion (A) and Reason (R) are true, but Reason (R) is the not the correct explanation of Assertion (A).
(c) Assertion (A) is false, but Reason (R) is true.
(d) Assertion (A) is true, but Reason (R) is false.

1. **Assertion** (A) International trade helps in speeding up the industrialisation of a country.

Reason (R) Developing countries export scarce raw materials and capital goods and advanced technology required for rapid industrial development.
Ans. (d) Developing countries import scarce raw materials and capital goods and advanced technology required for rapid industrial development.

2. **Assertion** (A) International trade helps people to improve their standard of living.

Reason (R) International trade helps people of a country to have access to a large variety of goods and services.
Ans. (a) Both Assertion (A) and Reason (R) are true and Reason (R) is the correct explanation of Assertion (A).

3. **Assertion** (A) Imports enable the country to ensure its sovereignty and territorial integrity.
Reason (R) A country can import food grains and other essential commodities to prevent starvation.
Ans. (d) Countries import equipment for its armed forces– Army, Air Force and Navy which enable them to ensure sovereignty and territorial integrity.

• Case Based MCQs

1. **Direction** *Read the following text and answer question no. (i) to (vi) on the basis of the same.*

Aman Woollen Ltd. a leading woollen items manufacturing company established 20 years ago by Aman, is well-known for its quality goods and consumers have high brand loyalty for its products especially shawls. The company was doing very well but due to riots, terrorism, unrest in the area for past 10 years their sales are consistently slashing down. To solve this problem, the marketing manager of the company suggested to explore the possibility of going international and to appoint wholesalers country wide. The financial manager supported his suggestion and informed that government is also providing subsidies and technical and marketing support to such export-oriented industries as international trade offers many benefits to the nation. They also believe that in other countries they would be able to charge more price than they are currently charging. This will lead to better business strength.

(i) Which of the following is not the benefit of foreign trade to a nation?
   (a) Economic growth
   (b) Earning of foreign exchange
   (c) Higher profits
   (d) Price stability

Ans. (d) Price stability

(ii) A wholesaler helps a manufacturer to enjoy economies of scale by
   (a) providing him market information
   (b) providing orders
   (c) bearing risk
   (d) providing financial support

Ans. (b) providing orders

(iii) International trade offers many benefits to the nation, one such benefit is that it provides a way out to intense competition in domestic market, which implies
   (a) winding up internal business
   (b) doing international business
   (c) doing technological upgradation
   (d) promotion of goods and services

Ans. (b) doing international business

(iv) International business includes which among the following?
   (a) Merchandise and service exports and imports
   (b) Licensing and franchising
   (c) Foreign investments
   (d) All of the above

Ans. (d) All of the above

(v) In international trade, when prices in the domestic market are low, firms cannot earn more profits by selling their products in those countries in which prices are high.
   (a) True   (b) False
   (c) Partially true   (d) None of these

Ans. (b) When prices in the domestic market are low, firms can earn more profits by selling their products in those countries in which prices are high. This is one of the benefits of international trade to the firms.

(vi) Which benefit of international trade to firm is highlighted in the line, "They also believe that in other countries they would be able to charge more price than they are currently charging. This will lead to better business strength"?
   (a) Improved Business Vision
   (b) Increased Capacity Utilisation
   (c) Prospects for Growth
   (d) Prospects for Higher Profits

Ans. (d) Prospects for Higher Profits

2. Direction *Read the following text and answer question no. (i) to (vi) on the basis of the same.*

When the Indian economy opened in 1991, Harsha decided to take advantage of the same and start a business at an international level. He is very good in making paper crafts and decided to monetise the same. He made lot of such crafts and sold them in the foreign countries. He hired few like-minded people and started a small firm.

By following the same practice of selling high-quality paper crafts in international markets, the firm earned lot of revenue. Firm started to cater to more clients and at a larger level production, costs declined.

People in other countries who would like these kinds of products but can't purchase due to unavailability are also helped by this kind of trade.

These people will have access to these products and can use for their home décor and even to ease out some of their tasks. This practice of selling in foreign market further helped the firm to increase the business when the domestic. In the process, the firm also achieved maximum utilization of the human resources and other small machines who earlier used to be working at below maximum production levels.

(i) Which advantage of international trade (to nation) is highlighted in the line, "He hired few like-minded people and started a small firm."?
   (a) Earning of foreign exchange
   (b) Better utilisation of resources
   (c) Improving growth prospects and employment potential
   (d) Increased standard of living

Ans. (c) Improving growth prospects and employment potential

(ii) Which advantage of international trade (to firms) is highlighted in the line, "By following the same practice of selling high-quality paper crafts in international markets, the firm earned lot of revenue."?

(a) Prospects for higher profits
(b) Way out to intense competition in domestic market
(c) Increased capacity utilisation
(d) Improved business vision

Ans. (a) Prospects for higher profits

(iii) Which advantage of international trade (to nation) is highlighted in the line, "People in other countries who would like these kinds of products but can't purchase due to unavailability are also helped by this kind of trade."?

(a) Speed-up industrialisation
(b) Meet consumer demand
(c) Overcome famine
(d) Ensure national defense

Ans. (b) Meet consumer demand

(iv) Which advantage of international business (to nations) is highlighted in the line, "These people will have access to these products and can use for their home décor and even to ease out some of their tasks."?

(a) Earning of foreign exchange
(b) Better utilisation of resources
(c) Improving growth prospects and employment potential
(d) Increased standard of living

Ans. (b) Increased standard of living

(v) Which advantage of international business (to firm) is highlighted in the line, "This practice of selling in foreign market further helped the firm to increase the business when the domestic."?

(a) Prospects for higher profits
(b) Increased capacity utilisation
(c) Prospects for growth
(d) Improved business vision

Ans. (c) Prospects for growth

(vi) Which advantage of international business (to firm) is highlighted in the line, "In the process, the firm also achieved maximum utilisation of the human resources and other small machines who earlier used to be working at below maximum production levels."?

(a) Prospects for higher profits
(b) Increased capacity utilisation
(c) Prospects for growth
(d) Improved business vision

Ans. (b) Increased capacity utilisation

PART 2
Subjective Questions

• Short Answer (SA) Type Questions

1. What do you mean by international trade? Explain in brief. Also, how are transactions related to international trade settled?

Ans. International trade is the component of international business. It comprises of buying and selling of goods and services beyond the geographical borders of the country. It involves not only the international movement of goods and services, but also of capital, personnel, technology and intellectual property like patents, trademarks, copyright, etc. It is also referred to as 'foreign trade' or 'external trade'. It can also be understood as exchange of goods and services between residents of different countries. It involves the use of foreign exchange to discharge trade obligations and settle the transactions.

2. Patel Ltd. is a reputed company in the field of garments manufacturing in India. The company manufactures superior quality products. But the management is worried about its future prospects. The company is facing certain problems

(a) The domestic prices of its garments are low.
(b) Under-utilisation of capacity.
(c) Demand for garments is saturated in domestic market.

A meeting is called by the BoD to discuss the matter. The members arrived at a conclusion that internationalisation of business is the final solution to the problems faced by the company. Such internationalisation will result in the benefits to the company.

The company believes in assuming social responsibility. Hence, it also favoured 'internationalisation of business' as it will also lead to benefits for the question's nation. On the basis of above case, answer the following questions

(i) Define international business.
(ii) Write any one benefit of international business each to the nation and firm.

Ans. (i) Manufacturing and trading beyond the boundaries of one's own country is known as international or external business.

(ii) One benefit of international business to the nation is **Earning of Foreign Exchange** International business helps a country to earn foreign exchange which can be used to import capital goods, technology, petroleum products, etc. which are not available in the country or are relatively costlier if produced domestically.

One benefit of international business to the firm is **Higher Profits** Generally, international business is more beneficial than the domestic business. When the domestic prices are not satisfactory, business firms can earn more profits by selling their products in the international markets where prices are higher.

3. Foreign trade does not only help the macroeconomic variables and national economies at large but also firms importing and exporting goods and services. With reference to the statement, explain the benefits of international trade to the firms.

Ans. Following are the benefits of international trade to the firms

(i) **Improved Business Vision** Most enterprises have an urge to grow, to become more competitive, to diversify and derive the benefits of going global through international trade.

(ii) **Prospects for Growth** When the domestic demand for a firm's products or services start getting saturated in the domestic market, then firms can considerably improve prospects of their growth by venturing out in the international market.

(iii) **Way Out to Intense Competition in Domestic Market** Highly competitive domestic market drives many companies to go international in search of markets for their products.

(iv) **Increased Capacity Utilisation** Many business and industrial enterprises have unused capacity, that can be efficiently utilised for further production. Thus, surplus production can be used to generate extra profits from foreign trade.

4. Differentiate between domestic and international business on the following basis

(i) Nationality of buyers and sellers
(ii) Nationality of other shareholders
(iii) Political system and risks
(iv) Business regulations and policies

Ans. Difference between Domestic and International Business

Basis	Domestic Business	International Business
Nationality of Buyers and Sellers	People or organisations from one nation participate in domestic business transactions.	People or organisations of different countries participate in international business transactions.
Nationality of other Stakeholders	Various other stakeholders such as suppliers, employees, middlemen, shareholders and partners are usually citizens of the same country.	Various other stakeholders such as suppliers, employees, middlemen, shareholders and partners are from different nations.
Political System and Risks	Domestic business is subject to political system and risks of one single country.	Different countries have different forms of political systems and different degrees of risks which often become a barrier to international business.
Business Regulations and Policies	Domestic business is subject to rules, laws and policies, taxation system, etc., of a single country.	International business transactions are subject to rules, laws and policies, tariffs and quotas, etc. of multiple countries.

• Long Answer (LA) Type Questions

1. What are the reasons for growing popularity of international trade in the modern times?

Ans. The reasons for the growing popularity of international trade are

(i) **Natural Resources are Unevenly Distributed** The natural resources are unevenly distributed throughout the world. Some countries are rich in certain resources while other countries in certain other resources. The countries produce goods according to the availability of naturally occurring resources and then sell these to other countries. They also buy the goods produced by some other country, as per their need.

(ii) **Availability of Factors of Production** Factors of production, viz. land, labour and capital differ from country to country. Because of this, different countries produce different goods and then trade amongst themselves.

(iii) **Specialisation** Certain countries specialise in the production of certain specific goods. e.g., India specialises in the production of handicrafts. So, handicraft goods are exported from India.

(iv) **Cost Benefits** The cost of production of goods and services differ from country to country due to difference in geographical, socio-economical and political environment. Some countries can produce goods economically as compared to other countries, thus leading to international trade. For example, China can produce electronic goods cheaply. Because of this, other countries import electronic goods from China.

2. International business has entered into a new era of reforms. India too did not remain cut-off from these developments. India was under a severe debt trap and was facing crippling balance of payment crisis. In 1991, it approached the International Monetary Fund (IMF) for raising funds to tide over its balance of payment deficits. IMF agreed to lend money to India subject to the condition that India would undergo structural changes to be able to ensure repayment of borrowed funds. India had no alternative but to agree to the proposal. It was the very conditions imposed by IMF which more or less forced India to liberalise its economic policies. Since then a fairly large amount of liberalisation at the economic front has taken place. Though the process or reforms have somewhat slowed down, India is very much on the path to globalisation and integrating with the world economy.

While, on the one hand, many Multinational Corporations (MNCs) have ventured into Indian market for selling their products and services. Many Indian companies too have stepped out of the country to market their products and services to consumers in foreign countries.

(i) As per the given case, what do you understand by 'globalisation' and 'liberalisation'?

(ii) IMF forced India to make structural changes so that international trade is encouraged. Do you think that encouraging international trade is good for the country?   **(NCERT)**

Ans. (i) **Globalisation** means integration of the economy of the country with the world economy.

Liberalisation means freedom from government regulations in a country to allow for private sector companies to operate business transactions with fewer restrictions.

(ii) Yes, I think that encouraging international trade is beneficial for the country. It provides following benefits to a nation

(a) **Earning of Foreign Exchange** International trade helps countries to earn foreign exchange. This helps a country to import those goods and services which it cannot produce efficiently.

(b) **Better Utilisation of Resources** Since, countries tend to produce goods in which they have a comparative advantage, wasteful duplication of resources is prevented and they end up producing more.

(c) **Improving Growth Prospects and Employment Potential** Many countries follow the principle 'export and flourish' and improve their growth prospects, thereby, creating employment opportunities for their citizens.

(d) **Increased Standard of Living** International trade helps people of a country to have access to a large variety of goods and services. This helps them to improve their standard of living.

Chapter Test

Multiple Choice Questions

1. Many countries follow the principle .... and improve their growth prospects, thereby, creating employment opportunities for their citizens.
   (a) import and earn   (b) export and earn   (c) import and flourish   (d) export and flourish

2. Pick the odd one out
   (a) International trade   (b) Import trade   (c) Foreign trade   (d) External trade

3. In International business, the degree of mobility of factors of production like labour and capital across nations is relatively ..... .
   (a) equal   (b) less   (d) high   (d) can't be determined

4. **Statement I** Countries exchange their surplus production with goods that they are in excess supply in their country.

   Statement II Companies engage in international business so as to import available resources from other countries at higher prices and export goods on which they can fetch better prices.

   Alternatives
   (a) Statement I is correct and Statement II is wrong   (b) Statement II is correct and Statement I is wrong
   (c) Both the statements are correct   (d) Both the statements are incorrect

Short Answer (SA) Type Questions

1. How does international trade help in stabilising the prices of a product?

2. How does international trade help nations to improve on economic variables such as employment, foreign exchange and efficient utilisation of resources?

3. **Tourism and transportation** have emerged as major components of international trade in services. Most of the airlines, shipping companies, travel agencies and hotels get their major share of revenues from their overseas customers and operations abroad. Several countries have come to heavily depend on services as an important source of foreign exchange earnings and employment. India, for example, earns a sizeable amount of foreign exchange from exports of services related to travel and tourism.

   Business services When one country provides services to other country and in the process earns foreign exchange, this is also treated as a form of international business activity. Fee received for services like banking, insurance, rentals, engineering and management services form part of country's foreign exchange earnings. Undertaking of construction projects in foreign countries is also an example of export of business services. The other examples of such services include overseas management contracts where arrangements are made by one company of a country which provides personnel to perform general or specialised management functions for another company in a foreign country in lieu of the other country. **(NCERT)**

   (i) Is international trade related to only goods?

   (ii) Enumerate the different services which are traded internationally.

4. Mention any four points that differentiate domestic business from international business.

Long Answer (LA) Type Questions

1. What do you mean by International trade? How does it help the firms?

2. International trade helps the world at a larger level. For instance, country X produces certain grains more than anywhere else in the world because of nutrients present in its soil. It produces so much that even after self-consumption in country, they have some quantity left so they export to countries where there is shortage of those grains. This also helps in creating harmony and cooperation between the countries. With increasing demand for these high-quality grains all over the world, the country started to produce at larger level by making utilisation of resources better. Consequently, lot of people got involved in production and export of such grains leading to overall prosperity levels in the country.

   Identify and state the objectives of international trade highlighted in the passage by quoting the lines.

Answers

Multiple Choice Questions

1. (d)   *2. (b)*   *3. (b)*   *4. (d)*

For Detailed Solutions

Scan the code

Practice Papers
1-3

Practice Paper 1*
(Solved)

Instructions

■ Time : 2 Hours
■ Max. Marks : 40

1. The question paper contains three sections A, B and C.
2. Section A has Case Based Question, which has 5 MCQs, each question carrying 1 mark. .
3. Section B has 5 Short Answer Type Questions, each question carrying 3 marks.
4. Section C has 4 Long Answer Type Questions, each question carrying 5 marks.
5. There is no overall choice. However, internal choices have been provided in some questions. Student have to attempt only one of the alternatives in such questions.

As exact Blue-print and Pattern for CBSE Term II exams is not released yet. So the pattern of this paper is designed by the author on the basis of trend of past CBSE Papers. Students are advised not to consider the pattern of this paper as official, it is just for practice purpose.

Section A

This section consists of 5 MCQs based on a case study

Case Based MCQs (1 × 5 = 5 Marks)

PT and Sons is a shop in Chennai, Tamil Nadu. It purchases relatively small quantity of goods from different wholesalers and sell them to ultimate consumers. PT and Sons remain in direct and constant touch with the buyers, so they give important market information about the tastes, preferences and attitudes of customers to the wholesalers. It is also famous for keeping stock of a variety of products. This enables the consumers to make their choice. Over the time, its sales increased and it has got lot of capital. So, the owners decided to invest this capital and start trading the products in International markets as well. They believe that they will procure goods in which they have a comparative advantage, similarly manufacturers will produce goods in which they have comparative advantage and wasteful duplication of resources will be prevented. PT and Sons is known to have supreme quality of products which are not available in International markets. Through this international trade, countries will get access to a large variety of goods of PT and Sons.

1. In which type of internal trade, PT and Sons is involved in?
(a) Wholesale Trade   (b) Retail Trade   (c) Both of these   (d) None of these

2. Which service of retailers to wholesalers is highlighted in the line, "PT and Sons remain in direct and constant touch with the buyers, so they give important market information about the tastes, preferences and attitudes of customers to the wholesalers."?
(a) Collecting Market Information   (b) Help in Distribution of Goods
(c) Help in Promotion   (d) Enabling Large-scale Operations

3. Which service of retailers to consumers is highlighted in the line, "It is also famous for keeping stock of a variety of products. This enables the consumers to make their choice."?
(a) Wide Selection   (b) New Products Information
(c) Regular Availability of Products   (d) After Sale Services

4. Which advantage of international trade to nation is highlighted in the line, "They believe that they will procure goods in which they have a comparative advantage, similarly manufacturers will produce goods in which they have comparative advantage and wasteful duplication of resources will be prevented."?
(a) Earning of Foreign Exchange
(b) Better Utilisation of Resources
(c) Improving Growth Prospects and Employment Potential
(d) Increased Standard of Living

5. Which advantage of international trade to nation is highlighted in the line, "Through this international trade, countries will get access to a large variety of goods of PT and Sons."?
(a) Earning of Foreign Exchange
(b) Better Utilisation of Resources
(c) Improving Growth Prospects and Employment Potential
(d) Increased Standard of Living

Section B

This section consists of 5 questions of short answer type.

Short Answer Type Questions (3 Marks)

6. Glenn started his firm manufacturing textiles in a small city in Gujarat. It was a small firm which manufactured gloves and socks. Majority of the work was done by hands. As the demand for his goods increased, he decided to purchase small machines. However, he found that he was short of capital. He pondered and approached an organisation which helped him to get supplies of imported machines on hire-purchase schemes. Identify the institutional support highlighted here and state its other functions.

7. Mention any three points of difference between American Depository Receipts (ADRs) and Global Depository Receipts (GDRs).

Or

What is the meaning of trade credit? Also, explain the factors on which trade credit depends upon.

8. How do Small Scale industries help in supply of various goods and involve low cost of production?

9. Retained earnings means that part of trading profits which are not distributed in the form of dividends, but retained by directors for future expansion of the company. In the light of statement, write any three merits and three demerits of retained earnings.

Or

The financial needs of the business can be categorised into fixed capital requirements and working capital requirements. Write the meaning and two features of both fixed capital requirements and working capital requirements.

10. For a developing economy like India, there is a desperate need of entrepreneurship development. Why?

Or

Intellectual property rights are the intellectuals emerged from the human mind and the legal right on these human intellects. In the light of the statement, explain the importance of Intellectual rights in detail.

Section C

This section consists of 4 questions of long answer type.

Long Answer Type Questions (5 Marks)

11. Commercial banks such as State Bank of India (SBI), Canara Bank, etc, advance money to the business firms for different purposes and different time periods. What are the merits and demerits of such finance?

Or

The government has established a number of financial institutions all over the country to provide finance to business organisations. These institutions are established by the Central as well as State Governments. What are the merits and demerits of such finance?

12. Beauty House is a wholesaler in Meerut district of Uttar Pradesh dealing in Beauty products. It purchases products from multiple manufacturers and make them available to retailers. Since, the orders are of big-ticket size, at times, it allows the retailers to take goods on pay later basis. It even takes some advertising and promotional events to increase the secondary and tertiary sale in the market. It also inform the retailers about various new products, schemes and qualities of these products.

The given text talks about multiple services offered by wholesalers to retailers. Highlighting the lines, identify and explain any three those services.

13. AMCD stores try to maximise customer satisfaction by providing additional facilities such as restaurants, travel and information bureau, free wi-fi zone, kids zone, rest rooms, etc. Identify the type of store and explain its advantages.

Or

OPQR stores have got many stores in the country. The price of the goods is fixed and sales are made on cash basis. Daily sales are deposited in a local bank account and details to this regard are sent to the head office. Identify the type of stores and explain its advantages.

14. Differentiate between domestic business and international business on any five basis.

Or

What do you understand by the term international business. State any three of its advantages to the firm.

Answers

1. (ba) Retail Trade

2. (a) Collecting Market Information

3. (a) Wide Selection

4. (b) Better Utilisation of Resources

5. (d) Increased Standard of Living

6. The institutional support highlighted here is National Small Industries Corporation (NSIC).

The functions are

(i)   It launches various schemes and extends support to help small scale entrepreneurs.

(ii) It exports the product of small units and help to establish their credit worthiness.

(iii) It helps in upgradation of technology.

(iv) It provides mentoring and advisory services.

(v) It serves as technology business incubator.

(vi) It develops software technology parks and technology transfer centres.

7. The following differences are observed between the two stated instruments

(i)   American Depository Receipts (ADR) can be bought and sold only in America, whereas Global Depository Receipts (GDR) can be bought and sold in many international markets.

(ii) Issue of ADRs require strict disclosure requirements, whereas issue of GDRs do not require strict disclosure requirements.

(iii) ADRs are more liquid, whereas GDRs are less liquid.

Or

Trade credit facilitates the purchase of supplies and raw material without immediate payment. Such credit appears in the accounts of the buyer of goods as sundry creditors or accounts payable. It is commonly used by business organisation as a source of short-term financing.

The amount and period of trade credit depends on the following factors

(i) Goodwill or reputation of the purchasing firm.

(ii) The amount of purchases made.

(iii) Past record of the buyer and his financial position. Also, the terms to trade credit may vary from industry to industry and person to person.

8. Small scale industries justify the mentioned qualities as follows

(i) **Supply Variety of Products** Small industries in our country supply enormous variety of products which include goods of mass consumption such as readymade garments, hosiery goods, stationery items, soaps and detergents, domestic utensils, etc. Sophisticated goods such as electrical goods, engineering goods, drugs, etc are also manufactured by these industries.

(ii) **Low Cost of Production** They also enjoy the advantage of low cost of production. This is because the establishment and running costs are minimal. Locally available resources are also less expensive. Due to lower cost of production, they have competitive strength.

9. Merits of Retained Earnings are

(i) Retained earnings are permanent source of funds for an organisation.

(ii) Retained earnings do not involve any explicit cost in the form of interest, dividend or floatation cost.

(iii) This source offers a greater degree of operational freedom and flexibility.

Demerits of Retained Earnings are

(i) Excessive ploughing back may cause dissatisfaction amongst the shareholders, as they would get lower dividends.

(ii) As the profits of business are fluctuating, it is an uncertain source of fund.

(iii) Firms do not recognise the opportunity cost associated with this source, leading to sub-optimal use of funds.

Or

The amount which is required to purchase fixed assets is known as fixed capital requirements of the enterprise. Features of fixed capital requirements are(any two)

(i) Fixed capital requirements are more for a manufacturing firm as compared to a trading firm.

(ii) Fixed capital requirements are more for a business operating on a large scale.

(iii) Fixed capital requirements should be financed through long-term sources of finance.

The amount required to meet these needs is known as the working capital requirements of the business. Features of working capital requirements are (any two)

(i) The shorter the operating cycle, the lesser will be the amount of working capital required and vice-versa.

(ii) Working capital requirements are generally met through short-term sources of finance.

(iii) Working capital requirement for a business selling goods on credit or having slow sales turnover is more than otherwise.

10. Need of entrepreneurship development arises due to the following reasons

(i) **More Utilisation of Natural Resources** It enables the economy to utilise and explore the abundant of natural resources.

(ii) **Economic Growth and Development** It provides the base of industrialisation in economy which is the main cause of economic growth and economic development

(iii) **Capital Formation** It encourages the establishment of new industries in economy which increase the capital formation rate in country.

(iv) **Development of Backward and Tribal Areas** It leads to scattering of economic activities in all areas of the country.

Or

Importance of Intellectual Property Rights is

(i) Exclusive right on the use of IP is the biggest motivation behind creation of intellectual property.

(ii) Customers get improved goods and services due to IPR.

(iii) Entrepreneurs are enabled to earn more revenue due to IPR.

(iv) It is cost saving mechanism for society through effectively utilisation of resources.

11. Merits of commercial institutions are

(i) Banks provide timely assistance to business by providing funds as and when needed.

(ii) Secrecy of business can be maintained as the information supplied to the bank by the borrowers is kept confidential.

(iii) Formalities such as issue of prospectus and underwriting are not required for raising loans from a bank. This, therefore, is an easier source of funds.

Demerits of commercial institutions are

(i) Funds are generally available for short periods and its extension or renewal is uncertain and difficult.

(ii) Banks make detailed investigation of the company's affairs, financial structure, etc. This makes the procedure of obtaining funds slightly difficult.

(iii) In some cases, difficult terms and conditions are imposed by banks for the grant of loan.

Or

Merits of financial institutions are

(i) Financial institutions provide long-term finance that is not provided by the commercial banks.

(ii) These institutes not only provide funds but also extend technical and managerial support to business firms.

(iii) Only a promising and sound business is able to get a loan from these institutions. So, if a firm gets a loan from these institutes, then this will also help in raising the goodwill of the borrowing company in the capital market.

Demerits of financial institutions are

(i) Too many formalities are required by these institutes to grant a loan.

(ii) Restrictions are imposed by these institutes on companies such as restrictions on the payment of dividends or restrictions on the autonomy of management.

(iii) Generally, the financial institutions have their nominees in the Board of Directors of the borrowed company. This restricts their powers and the borrowed companies feel helpless in certain cases.

12. Following services are highlighted in the case (any three)

(i) **Availability of Goods** The wholesalers make the products of various manufacturers readily available to the retailers. Because of this, the retailers are able to offer a variety of goods to their customers.

   Line " It purchases products from multiple manufacturers and make them available to retailers."

(ii) **Marketing Support** The wholesalers perform various marketing functions such as advertisement and other sales promotional activities to induce customers to purchase the goods. This increases the demand of the products which results in increased profits for the retailer.

   Line "It even takes some advertising and promotional events to increase the secondary and tertiary sale in the market."

(iii) **Grant of Credit** The wholesalers generally extend credit facilities to retailers. This enables them to manage their business with relatively small amount of working capital.

   Line *"Since, the orders are of big-ticket size, at times, it allows the retailers to take goods on pay later basis"*

(iv) **Specialised Knowledge** The wholesalers specialise in one line production. They inform the retailers about the new products, their uses, quality, prices, etc.

   Line "They also inform the retailers about various new products, schemes and qualities of these products."

13. The type of store mentioned is departmental stores. Its advantages are

(i) **Attract Large Number of Customers** As these stores are centrally located, therefore they attract a large number of customers.

(ii) **Convenience in Buying** These stores offer a large variety of goods under one roof. Therefore, it is convenient for customers to purchase goods from these stores.

(iii) **Attractive Services** These stores provide extra services to the customers, such as, home delivery of goods, accepting orders through telephone and online, provision of rest rooms, restaurants, etc.

(iv) **Economy of Large-scale Operations** These stores are organised and managed on a large scale. Therefore, they are able to enjoy economies of large scale operations and increase their profits.

(v) **Promotion of Sales** The departmental stores are in a position to spend considerable amount of money on advertising and other promotional activities which help in boosting the sales.

Or

The type of store mentioned is Chain stores. Its advantages are (any five)

(i) **Economies of Scale** These stores also operate on a high scale and procure the goods centrally. Therefore, they are also able to enjoy economies of scale.

(ii) **Elimination of Middlemen** Through these stores, the manufacturers sells goods directly to the consumers, thus eliminating unnecessary middlemen in the sale and purchase of goods.

(iii) **No Bad Debts** All the sales in these stores are made in cash. Therefore, there is no question of bad debts.

(iv) **Transfer of Goods** In case of lack of demand, goods from one store can be transferred to another store.

(v) **Diffusion of Risk** The risk is spread over a number of shops. Loss from one shop can be recovered from the profit of another shop.

(vi) **Low Cost** Because of centralised purchasing, elimination of middlemen and centralised promotion of sales, chain stores have low operational costs.

14. Difference between domestic business and international business is as follows (Any five)

Basis	Domestic Business	International Business
Nationality of Buyers and Sellers	People or organisations from one nation participate in domestic business transactions.	People or organisations of different countries participate in international business transactions.
Nationality of Other Stakeholders	Various other stakeholders such as suppliers, employees, middlemen, shareholders and partners are usually citizens of the same country.	Various other stakeholders such as suppliers, employees, middlemen, share holders and partners are from different nations.
Mobility of Factors of Production	The degree of mobility of factors of production like labour and capital is relatively more within a country.	The degree of mobility of factors of production like labour and capital across nations is relatively less.
Customer Heterogeneity across Markets	Domestic markets are relatively more homogeneous in nature.	International markets lack homogeneity due to differences in language, preferences, customs, etc., across markets.
Differences in Business Systems and Practices	Business systems and practices are relatively more homogeneous within a country.	Business systems and practices vary considerably across countries.
Political System and Risks	Domestic business is subject to political system and risks of one single country.	Different countries have different forms of political systems and different degrees of risks which often become a barrier to international business.

Or

Manufacturing and trading beyond the boundaries of one's own country is known as international business. It can be defined as those business activities that take place across the national frontiers.

Its advantages to firms are (any three)

(i) Many business and industrial enterprises have unused capacity, that can be efficiently utilised for further production. Thus, surplus production can be used to generate extra profits from foreign trade.

(ii) Highly competitive domestic market drives many companies to go international in search of markets for their products.

(iii) When prices in the domestic market are low, firms can earn more profits by selling their bucts in those countries in which prices are high.

(iv) When the domestic demand for a firm's product or services start getting saturated in the domestic market, then firms can considerably improve prospects of their growth by venturing out in the international market.

Practice Paper 2* (Solved)

Instructions

- Time : 2 Hours
- Max. Marks : 40

1. The question paper contains three sections A, B and C.
2. Section A has Case Based Question, which has 5 MCQs, each question carrying 1 mark. .
3. Section B has 5 Short Answer Type Questions, each question carrying 3 marks.
4. Section C has 4 Long Answer Type Questions, each question carrying 5 marks.
5. There is no overall choice. However, internal choices have been provided in some questions. Student have to attempt only one of the alternatives in such questions.

*** As exact Blue-print and Pattern for CBSE Term II exams is not released yet. So the pattern of this paper is designed by the author on the basis of trend of past CBSE Papers. Students are advised not to consider the pattern of this paper as official, it is just for practice purpose.**

Section A

This section consists of 5 MCQs based on a case study

Case Based MCQs ($1 \times 5 = 5$ Marks)

WS limited is a wholesaler situated in Bangalore, Karnataka. It is managed by two brothers- Venky & Kartik. It serves as an important link between manufacturers and retailers. It takes delivery of the goods and keeps them in large lots in its warehouse. In this process, it helps the manufacturer a lot. After that it supplies goods to the retailers. Interestingly, WS limited do not ask for the payment immediately. This enables the retailers to manage their business with relatively small working capital. These retailers are the last step in the value chain and create place utility. These retailers make the goods available to the final consumers who purchase them and use them for their consumption. To further increase their income, the brothers have decided to open up a new store. The store will be a large establish- ment offering a wide variety of products which are dealt by WS limited only. However, the store will have products of multiple brands and not just one particular brand.

1. Which service of wholesaler to manufacturer is highlighted in the line, "It serves as an important link between manufacturers and retailers. It takes delivery of the goods and keeps them in large lots in its warehouse"?

(a) Facilitating Large Scale Production
(b) Bearing Risk
(c) Financial Assistance
(d) Help in the Marketing Function

2. Which service of wholesaler to retailer is highlighted in the line, "WS limited do not ask for the payment immediately. This enables the retailers to manage their business with relatively small working capital."?

(a) Availability of Goods
(b) Marketing Support
(c) Grant of Credit
(d) Risk Sharing

3. Which service of retailer to manufacturer is highlighted in the line, "These retailers make the goods available to the final consumers who purchase them and use them for their consumption."?

(a) Help in Distribution of Goods
(b) Personal Selling
(c) Enabling Large-scale Operations
(d) Collecting Market Information

4. Which type of stores is highlighted in the line, "The store will be a large establishment offering a wide variety of products which are dealt by WS limited only. However, the store will have products of multiple brands and not just one particular brand"?
(a) Departmental stores   (b) Chain stores
(c) Both of these   (d) None of these

5. Which type of trade is highlighted in the paragraph?
(a) Internal trade   (b) International trade
(c) Both of these   (d) None of these

Section B

This section consists of 5 questions of short answer type.

Short Answer Type Questions (3 Marks)

6. Departmental stores are large establishments offering a wide variety of products, classified into well-defined departments. In reference to the statement, state the features of departmental stores.

Or

One of the disadvantages of chain stores is that majority of the multiple shops deal only in limited range of products. For example, Reebok deals in sports-wear and foot wear. These stores do not sell products of other manufacturers. Therefore, customers visiting these stores have only selected items to choose from. There are more such disadvantages, explain any three of the same.

7. Jeetu is a retailer store owner dealing in stationery products. He has lot of experience in this particular industry now. He makes sure that all the products of different types and brands are available to customers. He is known for keeping a large variety of SKUs. He also educates the customers about the new product arrival and their uses. He even assists them in supplying them the refills of some of the products or even the repair of some medium to large items.

The above text talks about retailers' services to customers. By quoting the lines, explain three such services.

8. What do you mean by international trade? Explain how international trade helps nations in earning foreign exchange and increase the standard of living?

Or

Do you agree with the statement that "international business not only involve international movement of goods, but movement of few other things, too"? Also, explain how international trade helps firms in making way out to intense competition and improving the business vision?

9. Yash and Yashi were arguing whether international trade is actually necessary between the nations or is it just a fancy way to do business that gives no results. Help them in coming to a conclusion.

10. Explain the concept of trade. Also, explain the classification of trade.

Or

Explain the concept of international business. Also, define and explain the meaning of international trade as a part of international business.

Section C

This section consists of 4 questions of long answer type.

Long Answer Type Questions (5 Marks)

11. Write five points elaborating the role of small-scale industries in India.

Or

Mention about the following problems of small scale industries in India.
(i) Quality
(ii) Capacity Utilisation
(iii) Technology
(iv) Sickness
(v) Global Competition

12. Chetan Ltd is a public listed company in India listed on the stock exchanges in 2002. The company has maintained good Debt to Equity ratio till now. It has planned for expansion now and requires capital for the same. The company is considering the option which would help to maintain the ratio further and therefore, decides to raise funding through issue of shares. The company allotted shares in the following ways
(i) 20,00,000 shares were allotted to share-holders who were ready to take more risks from the company and to assume the voting rights.

(ii) 10,00,00 shares were allotted to shareholders who wanted to to receive dividend at a predetermined rate

Identify the types of shares highlighted and write merits of case (i) and demerits of case (ii).

Or

Ravi is a learning enthusiast person who loves to explore new applications and software. Seeing the upsurge of working dashboards to present data in an attractive manner, he learnt Power BI to the depth. He soon became a master in this tool and started an online business of teaching Power BI courses to the students and professionals. His teaching style was liked by many and word of mouth spread like wildfire. He started earning good and generated good revenues. He then decided to launch similar courses on tableau, Excel & PowerPoint. However, he felt that rather than using a third-party site which cuts a huge commission on his revenue, he should collate all the courses and launch on his own website. The cost of creation of his dynamic website was ₹ 1,00,000 plus the cost of hosting which is ₹ 20,000. Rather than seeking help from anyone else, he decided to invest all his revenue in the same and launched his website.

Identify the source of finance highlighted in the passage and write its merits and demerits.

13. Ishan is an inspirational boy who has always thought of solving the problems of this country. In his quest, he built a start-up which provided solutions for water pollution of the country. For a very long span of period, he worked on the model by using up his own savings. However, they soon reduced to almost nil making it difficult for him to continue. Fortunately, his model was highly appreciated by a leading CEO who decided to invest in the same from his own savings. Ishan started to refine his model and sell the same to some large authorities for mass implementation. To further expand, he decided to get funding from bank which involved the usual process of sharing the business plan and the valuation details. He still required some capital and therefore, reached to a professionally managed fund agencies who invest in companies that have huge potential in future.

Identify any four methods of start-up funding highlighted here by quoting the lines. Also, explain any two other methods available too.

14. What do you mean by public deposits? Mention its merits and demerits.

Or

Preference shares resemble debentures as they bear a fixed rate of return. Also, as the dividend is payable only at the discretion of the directors and only out of profit after tax, to that extent, they resemble equity shares. In the light of the statement, explain the merits and demerits of preference shares.

Answers

1. (b) Bearing Risk
2. (c) Grant of Credit
3. (a) Help in Distribution of Goods
4. (a) Departmental stores
5. (a) Internal trade
6. The following are the distinct features of departmental stores
   (i) These stores are centrally located so that they can cater to large number of customers.
   (ii) These stores try to maximise customer satisfaction by providing additional facilities such as restaurants, travel and information bureau, free wi-fi zone, kids zone, rest rooms, etc.
   (iii) These stores cater to that segment of customers for whom price is secondary.
   (iv) The form of organisation for such stores is joint stock companies managed by Board of Directors.
   (v) These stores purchase goods directly from the manufacturers and maintain their own warehouses where goods are stored. Thus, these stores combine the functions of retailing and selling.
   (vi) These stores have a centralised purchasing department, whereas sales are decentralised in different departments.

   Or

   Disadvantages of chain stores are
   (i) **Lack of Initiative** The employees working in these stores work on the instructions of the head office. Also, they do not stand to benefit in any way by the sales made by them. So, they do not take initiative on their own.
   (ii) **Lack of Personal Touch** Due to operating on a large scale and lack of initiative on the part of employees, their dealings with customers lack personal touch.
   (iii) **Loss Due to Change in Demand** If the demand for the goods sold by these stores change rapidly, then the management may have to sustain heavy losses, because of large stocks lying unsold at the central depot.

7. Services of retailers to customers highlighted in the case are (any three)
   (i) **Regular Availability of Products** The most important service of a retailer to consumers is to maintain regular availability of various products produced by different manufacturers.

   Line "He makes sure that all the products of different types and brands are available to customers."

   (ii) **New Products Information** By arranging effective display of products, retailers provide important information about the arrival, special features, etc of products to the customers.

   Line "He also educates the customers about the new product arrival and their uses."

   (iii) **Wide Selection** Retailers generally keep stock of a variety of products. This enables the consumers to make their choice.

   Line "He is known for keeping a large variety of SKUs."

   (iv) **After Sales Services** Retailers provide important after-sales services in the form of home delivery, supply of spare parts etc.

   Line "He even assists them in supplying them the refills of some of the products or even the repair of some medium to large items."

8. International trade comprises of buying and selling of goods and services beyond the geographical borders of the country. It is also referred to as 'foreign trade' or 'external trade'. It helps the nations in the following ways
   (i) **Earning of Foreign Exchange** International trade helps countries to earn foreign exchange. This helps a country to import those goods and services which it cannot produce efficiently.
   (ii) **Increased Standard of Living** International trade helps people of a country to have access to a large variety of goods and services. This helps them to improve their standard of living.

   Or

   Yes, I agree with the given statement. International business involves not only the international movement of goods and services, but also of capital, personnel, technology and intellectual property.

   International trade helps the nations in the following ways
   (i) **Way Out to Intense Competition in Domestic Market** Highly competitive domestic market drives many companies to go international in search of markets for their products.
   (ii) **Improved Business Vision** Most enterprises have an urge to grow, to become more competitive, to diversify and derive the benefits of going global through international trade.

9. Yash and Yashi can be brought to a conclusion that international trade is actually necessary between the nations because of the following reasons
   (i) **Uneven Distribution of Natural Resources** All the countries cannot produce equally or cheaply because of uneven distribution of natural resources among them as well as differences in

their productivity levels. Thus, contries exchange their surplus production with goods that they are in short supply in their country.

(ii) **Factors of Production Availability** Each country differ in terms of availability of various factors of production such as labour, capital and raw materials, needed for producing different goods and services.

(iii) **Specialisation of Products** Many countries specialise in the production of certain goods and services for which they have some advantages such as suitable climatic conditions, technical know how, high labour productivity, etc.

(iv) **Benefits of Cost** Cost of production differ in different countries due to different socio-economic, political and geographical conditions. Many of the countries are in a better position to produce some goods more economically than other countries. Thus, companies engage in international business so as to import available resources from other countries at lower prices and export goods on which they can fetch better prices.

10. Trade refers to buying and selling of goods and services with the objective of earning profit. It bridges the gap between the producer and the consumer. The importance of trade in modern times has increased, as new products are being developed every day and are being made available for consumption throughout the world.

Trade can broadly be classified into two categories

(i) **Internal Trade** Trade which takes place within a country is called internal trade.

(ii) **External Trade** Trade which takes place between two or more countries is called external trade.

Or

International business can be defined as manufacturing and trading beyond the boundaries of one's own country. It involves business activities that take place across the national frontiers. It involves not only the international movement of goods and services, but also of capital, personnel, technology and intellectual property like patents, trademarks, copyright, etc.

International trade is the component of International business. It comprises of buying and selling of goods and services beyond the geographical borders of the country. It is also referred to as 'foreign trade' or 'external trade'. It can also be understood as exchange of goods and services between residents of different countries. It involves the use of foreign exchange to discharge trade obligations.

11. Role of small scale industries in India can be understood with the help of following points (any five)

(i) **Contribution in GDP** Small industries in India account for 95% of the industrial units of the country. They contribute almost 40% of the gross industrial value added and 45% of the total exports (direct and indirect) from India.

(ii) **Employment Generation** In India, small industries are the second largest employers of human resources, after agriculture. They generate more employment opportunities per unit of capital invested as compared to large industries. Thus, they are considered good for countries like India, that have surplus labour and less capital.

(iii) **Supply Variety of Products** Small industries in our country supply enormous variety of products which include goods of mass consumption such as readymade garments, hosiery goods, stationery items, soaps and detergents, domestic utensils, etc. Sophisticated goods such as electrical goods, engineering goods, drugs, etc are also manufactured by these industries.

(iv) **Balanced Regional Development** As these industries produce products using simple technologies and depend on locally available resources in terms of both material and labour, thus, they can be opened anywhere in the country, without any locational constraints and the benefits of industrialisation can be reaped by every region.

(v) **Provide Business Opportunities** They provide ample opportunity for entrepreneurship. The latent skills and talents of people can be channelled into business ideas, which can be converted into reality with little or nil capital investment.

(vi) **Low Cost of Production** They also enjoy the advantage of low cost of production. This is because the establishment and running cost are minimal. Locally available resources are less expensive. Due to lower cost of production, they have competitive strength.

Or

(i) **Quality** Many small business organisations do not adhere to desired standards of quality. Instead, they concentrate on cutting the cost and keeping the prices low. As they do not maintain quality, they are not able to compete in global markets.

(ii) **Capacity Utilisation** Due to lack of marketing skills leading to lack of demand, many small business firms have to operate below full capacity due to which their operating costs tend to increase. This leads to sickness and closure of the business.

(iii) **Technology** Use of outdated technology is often stated as a serious problem of such enterprises. This results in low productivity and uneconomical production.

(iv) **Sickness** Prevalence of sickness in small industries has become a point of worry for both the policy-makers and the entrepreneurs. The causes of sickness are both internal and external.

  (a) Internal problems include lack of skilled and trained labour, managerial and marketing skills.

  (b) External problems include delayed payment, shortage of working capital, inadequate loans and lack of demand for their products.

(v) **Global Competition** In the present context of Liberalisation, Privatisation and Globalisation (LPG) policies being followed by several countries across the world. Small businesses feel threatened from the global entrepreneurs in the following areas

  (a) Competitions from medium and large industries as well as multinational companies.

  (b) High quality standards, technological skills, financial credit worthiness, managerial and marketing capabilities of large industries.

  (c) Due to strict requirements of quality certification like ISO 9000, small industries have limited access to markets of developed countries.

12. Case (i) 20,00,000 shares were allotted to shareholders who were ready to take more risks from the company and to assume the voting rights

Shares highlighted in this case are equity shares.

Merits of equity shares are (any three)

(i) Equity shares are suitable for those investors who are willing to assume risk for higher returns.

(ii) Payment of dividend to the equity shareholders is not compulsory. Therefore, there is no burden on the company.

(iii) It is considered as a good source of long-term finance. A company is not required to pay back the equity capital during its lifetime. It is repaid only at the time of liquidation of company. Also, since it is paid last, even on liquidation, therefore it provides a cushion for creditors. Thus, it is a permanent source of capital.

(iv) Equity capital provides credit worthiness to the company and confidence to prospective loan providers.

Case (ii) 10,00,00 shares were allotted to shareholders who wanted to to receive dividend at a predetermined rate.

Shares highlighted in this case are preference shares.

Demerits of Preference shares are (any three)

(i) Preference shares are not suitable for those investors who are willing to take risk and are interested in higher returns.

(ii) These shares dilute the claim of equity shareholders over the assets of the company.

(iii) The company has to pay higher rates of dividends to the preference shareholders as compared to interest on debentures.

(iv) The dividend on these shares is to be paid only when the company earns profit. Thus, the returns are not assured and they are unable to attract the investors.

Or

The source of finance highlighted here is retained earnings.

Merits of retained earnings are (any three)

(i) Retained earnings is a permanent source of funds for an organisation.

(ii) Retained earnings do not involve any explicit cost in the form of interest, dividend or floatation cost.

(iii) This source offers a greater degree of operational freedom and flexibility.

(iv) It enhances the capacity of business to absorb unexpected losses.

(v) It might lead to an increase in the market price of equity shares issued by the company.

Demerits of retained earnings are

(i) Excessive ploughing back may cause dissatisfaction amongst the shareholders, as they would get lower dividends.

(ii) As the profits of business are fluctuating, it is an uncertain source of fund.

(iii) Firms do not recognise the opportunity cost associated with this source, leading to sub-optimal use of funds.

13. The methods of start-ups funding highlighted in the passage are (any three)

(i) **Bootstrapping Start-up Business** It is known as self-funding. Entrepreneur can invest from their past saving or can get from family or friends. It is suitable only if the initial requirement is small.

    Line "For a very long span of period, he worked on the model by using up his own savings."

(ii) **Bank Loan** Funding from bank will involve the usual process of sharing the business plan and the valuation details, along with project report based on which the loan is sanctioned.

    Line "To further expand, he decided to get funding from bank which involved the usual process of sharing the business plan and the valuation details."

(iii) **Angel Funding** Angel investors take very early-stage business under their wing while venture capital or equity investors do not like to commit capital to tiny business.

    Line "Fortunately, his model was highly appreciated by a leading CEO who decided to invest in the same from his own savings."

(iv) **Venture Capital** Venture capitals are professionally managed funds who invest in companies that have huge potential in future. They focus on sale rather than profit of ventures. This type of funding is often obtained in exchange for an equity stake in business.

Line "….therefore, reached to a professionally managed funds who invest in companies that have huge potential in future."

Other ways to funding (any two)

(i) **Incubators** They provide professional services that facilitates the development of new business by providing resources, support and advice. In India, more than 50% of the incubators are located in universities indicating role of universities in supporting new start-ups. e.g.

 (a) Innovation and Entrepreneurship (SINE), IIT Mumbai

 (b) Technology Business Incubator IIT Delhi

(ii) **Accelerators** Accelerators are organisations that offer a range of support service and funding opportunities for startups. They provide capital and investment in return for start-up equity. They target set action to boost the development and growth of a startups. e.g.

 (a) Amity Innovation Incubator

 (b) IAN Business Incubator, Kyron

(iii) **Crowd Funding** Crowd sourced funding is a means of raising money for a creative project (i.e, music, film book). It is a collection of funds from multiple investors through social networking sites for a specific project.

14. Public deposits refer to the deposits that are raised by business organisations directly from the public. Under it, a company directly raises loans from the public, in the form of deposits for a fixed period of time at a fixed rate of interest.

Merits of public deposits are

(i) The procedure of obtaining deposits is simple and does not contain restrictive conditions.

(ii) Cost of public deposits is generally lower than the cost of borrowings from banks and other institutions.

(iii) Public deposits do not usually create any charge on the assets of the company.

Demerits of public deposits are

(i) New companies generally find it difficult to raise funds through public deposits.

(ii) It is an unreliable source of finance as the public may not respond when the company needs money.

(iii) Collection of public deposits may prove difficult, when the size of deposits required is large.

Or

Merits of preference shares are (any three)

(i) The dividends to be paid to the preference shareholders are fixed. This ensures the investors the security of fixed returns.

(ii) These shares are suitable for those investors who want fixed income with comparatively low risk.

(iii) It does not affect the control of equity shareholders. as these shares do not carry voting rights.

(iv) Payment of fixed dividends to preference shareholders enable a company to declare higher dividends for equity shareholders.

(v) The holders of these shares have a preferential right of repayment over equity shareholders, when the company liquidates.

(vi) Assets are not required to be mortgaged for raising preference share capital. Thus, the assets of the company are free from any charge and can be used to raise debt capital.

Demerits of preference shares are (any three)

(i) Preference shares are not suitable for those investors who are willing to take risk and are interested in higher returns.

(ii) These shares dilute the claim of equity shareholders over the assets of the company.

(iii) The company has to pay higher rates of dividends to the preference shareholders as compared to interest on debentures.

(iv) The dividend on these shares is to be paid only when the company earns profit. Thus, the returns are not assured and they are unable to attract the investors.

(v) The dividend paid on preference shares is not deductible from profits as expense. Thus, there is no tax savings, as in the case of interest on loans.

Practice Paper 3*
(Solved)

Instructions

■ Time : 2 Hours
■ Max. Marks : 40

1. The question paper contains three sections A, B and C.
2. Section A has Case Based Question, which has 5 MCQs, each question carrying 1 mark. .
3. Section B has 5 Short Answer Type Questions, each question carrying 3 marks.
4. Section C has 4 Long Answer Type Questions, each question carrying 5 marks.
5. There is no overall choice. However, internal choices have been provided in some questions. Student have to attempt only one of the alternatives in such questions.

** As exact Blue-print and Pattern for CBSE Term II exams is not released yet. So the pattern of this paper is designed by the author on the basis of trend of past CBSE Papers. Students are advised not to consider the pattern of this paper as official, it is just for practice purpose.*

Section A

This section consists of 5 MCQs based on a case study

Case Based MCQs (1 × 5 = 5 Marks)

Pragyan is a teenager with lot of entrepreneurial spirit. He has recently thought of an idea which can help people to detect the alcohol levels in the drinks accurately with the pocket size device. To further initiate the process he decided to register as a startup on the portal online. To do the research, he decided to use his own savings and complete the research. He could realise that his product was going to be a very bright product in the coming future therefore he decided to protect it with the help of an intellectual property right through the property right which gave him the exclusive right on that particular device that he invented. Now he wanted to purchase some machinery to get devices produced on a mass level. Since the amount was very big and he could not afford it by himself, he decided to take some money from commercial banks which were ready to provide him assistance because of his excellent idea.

1. Which Start up India Action point is highlighted in the line, "To further initiate the process he decided to register as a startup on the portal online."?
(a) Simplification & handholding
(b) Startup India Hub
(c) Easy Exit
(d) Tax Exemption

2. Which method of startup funding is highlighted in the line, "To do the research, he decided to use his own savings and complete the research."?
(a) Angel Investment
(b) Venture Capital
(c) Bootstrapping
(d) Microfinance

3. Which IPR gave him the exclusive right on the product?
(a) Copyright
(b) Trademark
(c) Trade Secrets
(d) Patent

4. Which type of working capital requirement is highlighted in the line, "Now he wanted to purchase some machinery to get devices produced on a mass level."?
(a) Fixed Capital
(b) Working capital
(c) Both of these
(d) None of these

5. Which type of funds are highlighted in the line, "he decided to take some money from commercial banks which were ready to provide him assistance because of his excellent idea."?

   (a) Owner's Fund
   (b) Borrowed Funds
   (c) Both of these
   (d) None of these

Section B

This section consists of 5 questions of short answer type.

Short Answer Type Questions (3 Marks)

6. State any three needs of finance for a business enterprise.

   Or

   Differentiate between internal and external source of business finance on the basis of

   (i) Purpose

   (ii) Cost

   (iii) Security required

7. Small scale industries are quintessential for providing employment in Rural India. Defend or refute the statement by giving two substantial arguments.

   Or

   Small scale industries are quintessential for industrialisation in Rural India and alleviating poverty thereof. Defend or refute the statement by giving two substantial arguments.

8. Identify and define the type of IPRs highlighted in the following examples
    (i) Telephone, radio, optical fibre, ipod and ballpoint pens.
    (ii) Original literary, dramatic, musical or artistic works, sound recording, films and broadcasts.
   (iii) MC Donald's double arches, apple Computer's, Apple sign of Android.

9. After the pandemic, India saw an upsurge in the number of start-ups that have come up the ranks and became unicorns. This clearly shows the entrepreneurial spirit in our country is enhancing with the passing time. How will entrepreneurship development help a developing economy like India? Explain any three ways in brief.

10. Some companies prefer to raise the money through the issue of debentures and not through the issue of equity shares. What could be the reasons for the same?

    Or

    Differentiate between equity shares and preference shares on the basis of
     (i) Participation in management
     (ii) Sequence of Dividend
    (iii) Sequence of Refund of capital

Section C

This section consists of 4 questions of long answer type.

Long Answer Type Questions (5 Marks)

11. Meena stores is a line of stores with multiple stores in west side of the country. These stores have similar arrangement and deal in standardised and branded consumer products, which have rapid sales turnover. Identify the type of fixed-shop large retailers and state its features.

    Or

    365*12 is a company with a big store in Kolkata, West Bengal. It aims at satisfying practically every customer's need under one roof. It has a number of departments, each one confining its activities to a specific kind of product. Identify the store highlighted here and state its disadvantages.

12. On an individual firm level, the international trade opens many new opportunities and prospects. In the light of the statement, explain any five advantages of international trade to the firms.

13. BPR is an outlet in MG Road area of Gurugram. It deals with FMCG products and keeps high quantity of the stocks of the same. It also maintains good number of varieties of the same. While purchasing the goods, it pays the manufacturers in cash and assists them in the marketing of the goods. It supplies goods to Ahuja Bros which is another outlet in the outskirts of Gurugram. It makes the goods available to the final consumer.

The text highlights two types of different internal trade. Identify and explain them. Also, mention which outlet falls in which type.

Or

Max enterprises is a wholesaler dealing in packed food products. It collects small orders from a number of retailers and passes on the pool of such orders to the manufacturers and makes purchases in bulk quantities and pays for the same in cash. Moreover, it stores a large quantity of stock in its warehouse to ensure supply as and when required. It also advises the manufacturers to produce different products according to the customer's tastes and preferences. With all these operations, it has been fairly successful in its operations.

Highlight the lines which reflect the services of wholesalers to manufacturers. Also, name those services and explain them.

14. Retail trade is performed by retailers. A retailer is engaged in the sale of goods and services directly to the ultimate consumers. Explain how consumers are benefitted by the consumers.

Or

Retailar performs a function of retail trade. He is engaged in the sale of goods and services directly to the ultimate consumers. Retailer represent the final stage in the distribution process. Explain how wholesalers/Manufacturers are benefitted by the retailers.

Answers

1. (a) Simplification & handholding

2. (c) Bootstrapping

3. (d) Patent

4. (a) Fixed Capital

5. (b) Borrowed Funds

6. Business enterprises require finance for the following reasons

  (i) For financing fixed capital requirements, i.e., purchase of land, building, plant and machinery, etc.

  (ii) For financing working capital requirements, i.e., purchase of raw material, payment of wages/salaries, for meeting certain expenditures, etc.

(iii) For growth and expansion of business enterprise.

Or

Difference between internal and external sources are

Basis	Internal Sources	External Sources
Purpose	The internal sources of funds can fulfil only limited needs of the business.	Large amount of money can be raised through external sources.
Cost	Cost of internal funds is low.	External funds are more costly.
Security Required	Business is not required to provide security while obtaining funds from internal sources.	Business is required to mortgage its assets as security while obtaining funds from external sources.

7. I agree with the statement that small scale industries are quintessential for providing employment in Rural India. The role of small business in rural India is explained in the following points

   (i) **Non-farm Employment** Traditionally, rural households in India were exclusively engaged in agriculture. But now, rural households have varied and multiple sources of income, and participate in a wide range of non-agricultural activities alongwith the traditional rural activities of farming and agricultural labour. This can be largely attributed to the setting up of agro-based rural small industries.

   (ii) **Employment for Artisans** Cottage and rural industries play an important role in providing employment opportunities in the rural areas, especially to the traditional artisans and the weaker sections of society.

Or

Yes, I agree with the statement that small scale industries are quintessential for industrialisation in Rural India and alleviating poverty thereof. The role of small business in rural India is explained in the following points

   (i) **Poverty Alleviation** Village and small industries are significant as producers of consumer goods and absorbers of surplus labour, thereby addressing the problems of supply, poverty and unemployment.

   (ii) **Promoting SSI and Rural Industrialisation** Promotion of small scale industries and rural industrialisation has been considered by the Government of India as a powerful instrument for realising the twin objectives of "accelerated industrial growth and creating additional productive employment potential in rural and backward areas."

8. (i) **Patent** as an exclusive right is granted in respect of an invention which may be product or process that provides a new and inventive way of doing something, or offers a new and inventive technical solution to a problem.

   (ii) **Copyright** is a legal right created by the law that grant the creator of an original work's exclusive rights for its use and distribution.

   (iii) **Trademark** provides recognisable sign, design or expression which identifies products or services of a particular source from those of others.

9. Entrepreneurship development helps a developing economy like India in the following ways (any three)

   (i) **Employment Opportunities** It enables entrepreneurs to create more/additional employment opportunities for youth.

   (ii) **Economic Independence** Entrepreneurs develop and produce substituted products of imported goods and prevent the over-dependence on the other countries.

   (iii) **Capital Formation** It encourages the establishment of new industries in economy which increase the capital formation rate in country.

   (iv) **Development of Backward and Tribal Areas** It leads to scattering of economic activities in all areas of the country.

10. Following are the advantages or reasons of issuing debentures instead of equity shares

   (i) Debentures are fixed charge funds and do not participate in the profits of the company.

   (ii) Financing through debentures does not dilute control of shareholders on management as debentures do not carry voting rights.

   (iii) Financing through debentures is less costly as compared to cost of equity capital as the interest payment on debentures is tax deductible.

Or

The differences between equity shares and preference shares are

Basis	Equity Shares	Preference Shares
Participation in Management	Full right to participate.	No right to participate.
Sequence of Dividend	Dividend is paid last of all.	Preference is given in payment of dividend.
Sequence of Refund of Capital	On winding up of the company, capital is refunded after preference shares.	Preference is given in refunding the capital.

11. The fixed-shop larger retailer highlighted in the given case is Chain Stores or Multiple shops.

The features of chain stores or multiple shops are

   (i) These shops are located in populous localities, so that customers can be served at a place near their residence.

   (ii) The manufacturing or procurement of merchandise for all the retail units is centralised.

(iii) Each retail outlet is under the direct supervision of a Branch Manager, who is responsible for its day-to-day operations.

(iv) All branches are controlled by the head office. The head office formulates policies and gets them implemented.

(v) The prices of the goods is fixed and sales are made on cash basis. Daily sales are deposited in a local bank account and details to this regard are sent to the head office.

(vi) The head office appoints inspectors, who supervise the day-to-day operations of the store in respect of quality of customer service provided, adherence to rules and regulations, etc.

Or

The store highlighted here is departmental store.

Disadvantages of departmental stores are

(i) **Lack of Personal Attention** Because of large scale operations, these stores are not able to give personal attention to each and every customer.

(ii) **High Operating Costs** Since these stores provide a number of additional services to their customers, therefore their operating costs are also high.

(iii) **High Possibility of Loss** These stores operate on large scale and incur high operating costs. Therefore, their exposure to risk is also high.

(iv) **Inconvenient Location** These stores are generally located in a central location. Customers encounter traffic problems while visiting these stores. Also, it is not convenient for the purchase of goods that are needed at short notice.

12. Advantages of international trade to the firms are

(i) **Prospects for Higher Profits** When prices in the domestic market are low, firms can earn more profits by selling their products in those countries in which prices are high.

(ii) **Prospects for Growth** When the domestic demand for a firm's product or services start getting saturated in the domestic market, then firms can considerably improve prospects of their growth by venturing out in the international market.

(iii) **Way Out to Intense Competition in Domestic Market** Highly competitive domestic market drives many companies to go international in search of markets for their products.

(iv) **Increased Capacity Utilisation** Many business and industrial enterprises have unused capacity, that can be efficiently utilised for further production. Thus, surplus production can be used to generate extra profits from foreign trade.

(v) **Improved Business Vision** Most enterprises have an urge to grow, to become more competitive, to diversify and derive the benefits of going global through international trade.

13. The two types of trades highlighted are

(i) **Wholesale Trade** It refers to purchasing goods and services in large quantity from manufacturers and reselling them to retailers, who then sells them to the ultimate consumers.

Chain of Wholesale Trade

Manufacturers —- Wholesalers —- Retailers —- Consumers

A wholesaler is an intermediary between manufacturer and retailer. Example: BPR

(ii) **Retail Trade** It refers to purchasing relatively small quantity of goods from wholesalers and selling them to ultimate consumers.

Chain of Retail Trade

Wholesalers —- Retailers —- Consumers

A retailer is an intermediary between wholesaler and consumer. Example: Ahuja Bros

Or

(i) **Facilitating Large Scale Production** Wholesalers collect small orders from a number of retailers and pass on the pool of such orders to the manufacturers and make purchases in bulk quantities. This enables the producers to undertake production on a large scale.

Line "It collects small orders from a number of retailers and passes on the pool of such orders to the manufacturers and makes purchases in bulk quantities...."

(ii) **Financial Assistance** They provide financial assistance to the manufacturers as they generally make cash payment for the goods purchased by them.

Line "..... and pays for the same in cash."

(iii) **Expert Advice** The wholesalers are in direct contact with the retailers, therefore they can advice the manufacturers about various aspects related to customer's tastes and preferences, market conditions, etc.

Line "It also advises the manufacturers to produce different products according to the customer's tastes and preferences."

(iv) **Storage** Wholesalers take delivery of goods when they are produced and keep them in their godowns/warehouses, thereby helping in storage of goods.

Line "Moreover, it stores a large quantity of stock in its warehouse to ensure supply as and when required."

14. Following are the services of retailers to the consumers (any five)

(i) **Regular Availability of Products** The most important service of a retailer to consumers is to maintain regular availability of various products produced by different manufacturers.

(ii) **New Products Information** By arranging effective display of products, retailers provide important information about the arrival, special features, etc of products to the customers.

(iii) **Convenience in Buying** Retailers generally sell goods in small quantities, according to the requirements of their customers. This offers great convenience to the customers.

(iv) **Wide Selection** Retailers generally keep stock of a variety of products. This enables the consumers to make their choice.

(v) **After Sales Services** Retailers provide important after-sales services in the form of home delivery, supply of spare parts etc.

(vi) **Provide Credit Facilities** The retailers sometimes provide credit facilities to their regular buyers, leading to increased level of consumption and better standard of living.

Or

Following are the services of retailers to the wholesaler/manufacturer

(i) **Help in Distribution of Goods** Retailers help in the distribution of products by making them available to the final consumers, thus, creating place utility.

(ii) **Personal Selling** By undertaking personal selling efforts, the retailers relieve the producers from this activity and greatly help them in the process of actualising the sale of the products.

(iii) **Enabling Large-scale Operations** On account of retailer's services, the manufacturers/wholesalers are freed from the botheration of making individual sales to consumers in small quantities.

(iv) **Collecting Market Information** As retailers remain in direct and constant touch with the buyers, they serve as an important source of collecting market information about the tastes, preferences and attitudes of customers.

(v) **Help in Promotion** Manufacturers and distributors carry on various promotional activities in order to increase the sale of their products. Retailers participate in these activities and help to promote the sale of the good.

Printed by Libri Plureos GmbH in Hamburg,
Germany